N&P
ASPECTS OF LIFE

CW00432412

Aspects of Life is a series of publications designed to help people to respond to the changing circumstances which they face as their lives progress.

In an entertaining and down-to-earth style the Aspects of Life Series seeks to encourage readers not only to tackle their responsibilities in a more fulfilling way, but also to enjoy the stimulus of new challenges.

The subject matter, which at present ranges through home life, leisure and work is being chosen to recognise the diversity of experience and opportunities which individuals and families may encounter.

This pioneering venture by a building society draws on N&P's unique experience in responding to customers' requirements, helping people to achieve a better quality of life.

First Published in Great Britain in 1993.

By N&P Publishing, a division of the National & Provincial Building Society, Provincial House, Bradford BD1 1NL, West Yorkshire.

© Frankie McGowan 1993.

Cover design by FKB Carlson, London.

Cover photography by Alwyn R. Coates.

Printed and bound in Great Britain by Lund Humphries Limited, Bradford.

Distributed by Book Point Ltd, 39 Milton Park, Abingdon, Oxford OX14 4TD.

Represented by John Wilson Booksales Ltd, 1 High Street, Princes Risborough, Buckinghamshire HP27 0AG.

British Library cataloguing in publication data record for this title is available from the British Library ISBN number 1 897634 03 X.

The contents of this publication are believed to be correct at time of printing. However, the publishers and author cannot accept responsibility for errors or omissions, nor for the changes in policy details given. Readers should always satisfy themselves that the facilities they require are available and that prices, where quoted, still apply.

WOMEN GOING
BACK TO WORK

iis book belor

FRANKIE McGOWAN

1993

To Mum, with love from all of us

Acknowledgments

No book ever gets under way without the co-operation and help of many people. So without whom…

I owe a real debt of gratitude to my brother, John McGowan, for his unflagging, invaluable help and support while I wrote this book. Very special thanks go to writer – and working mother – Helen Bullock, who compiled all the quizzes and inspired many thoughts along the way. Thanks, too, to Jayne Monkhouse at the Equal Opportunities Commission and Jo Gardiner at the Pepperell Network, who generously assisted me in my research. My grateful thanks, also, to Mary Hutchinson, who reminded me about the 'wonder years', and to Mary Tucker of the Citizens Advice Bureaux for her useful comments. Particular thanks and appreciation go to Maureen Storey for her meticulous research, Nicola Sherwell for some speedy checking and Sonya Taylor for patiently making sure it was all pulled together. Some very good mates – nearly all working mothers whose experiences over the years, of work and returning to work, have been invaluable in compiling this book – deserve my thanks. They include Penny Vincenzi, who 'returned' on the same day, Heather Forrester, who braved the PTA with me, and who remains a staunch ally, and Scarth Flett, who encouraged me when I 'returned'.

I am grateful in particular that Melanie Cantor, Sarah Meysey Thompson, Yvonne Roberts and Maggie Goodman are still, as they have always been, at the other end of the phone, and a special thank you must go to the remarkable Felicity Green, who helped so many of us through the tough times and pushed us on to start all over again. My working life would not have been quite so possible without the support of two special people, so affectionate thanks go to the incomparable Kathleen O'Donaghue and, later, Sharon Shoebridge, who were the rocks of my life.

Finally, my love and thanks to my children, Tom and Amy, and my husband, Peter Glossop, who, without doubt, are the real heroes of this book.

Frankie McGowan
London, 1993.

CONTENTS

INTRODUCTION

The time has come to ask yourself seriously whether or not you should return to work when:

a) You find yourself discussing Maastricht with your five-year-old
b) You desperately want to recall, just one more time, what it's like to go to the bathroom without a small child clinging to your leg
c) You want to eat lunch with people who don't behave as though everything that is green on their plate is poison
d) You want to hear a joke that doesn't begin, 'What do you get if you cross…'
e) You slip from mild curiosity about the nature of those who rob banks to wondering how easy it is.

Every year, come hell, recession or high water, thousands of women who've raised a family return, or consider returning, to the world of work. Why?
Why is it that so many who once regarded child rearing as sacrosanct, or whose original intention was to return to work straight from maternity leave but found, as the years slipped by, the very idea of work had become about as relevant to their lives as the rantings of a banana state dictator, suddenly discover they can think of little else but getting a job?
The motivations are surprisingly common: money, boredom – and independence.
There are also, of course, an increasing number of women, divorced, widowed, single parents, or those with spouses who have been made redundant, who do not have the luxury of choice and who would love to have nothing more to worry about than the routine of keeping a home together. They are the reluctant returners.
Only each individual woman knows why she's screwing up the courage to attempt the psychological leap ahead of her. But, whichever category she falls into, she is not alone.
Scores of guilt-stricken women suppress their anxieties about not 'being there' for their family when they reach this milestone in their lives, but there are even more who feel guilty about not exploiting

1

their earning power at a time when the family could do with the extra cash. There are women who so long for independence, both emotionally and financially, that they find themselves dreaming that Judy and Richard suddenly lose control and start hitting each other in the middle of This Morning, after which they divorce and thus restore a sense of adequacy to the rest of the nation's married women.

Many more women are generally resentful of being regarded simply as an appendage to their family ('Jeremy's wife' or 'William and Mary's mother'), are fed up with scrimping on themselves, of always having to think twice about buying a new pair of tights or resisting the temptation of the aisles stacked with anti-ageing creams. Most of all, they want to have the simple right to be their own person and to be treated as an equal.

Working mothers – or indeed any women returning to the workplace after a significant break – no longer make the news. That they are no longer regarded as a special cateogory is no bad thing. But, equally, it means that what are now largely being ignored are the terrors and traumas of returning to a world stocked with technology and bright young things with degrees in New Age subjects like media studies or communications, and who can operate a range of computer programmes without a flicker of doubt invading their minds when the average returner would be hard put to find the 'on' switch.

This is where this book comes in. High-flyers and those with wealth and connections are kindly requested to talk quietly among themselves, but for the thousands of others with energy, enthusiasm and a lot to offer, but who can't find the arrow which says, 'This way to the bossy, bitchy, brave new world of work', read on.

Books galore have been written about women returners, but they largely restrict themselves to learning new office skills and how to get promotion. While this book takes those subjects seriously, it is not exclusively devoted to upward mobility. Its purpose is to sweep aside the myth of the power suit, the power lunch and the politically correct way to address co-workers and management, and to get on with the real business of what working is all about.

Which means, as all of us who have done it can tell you, coping with family dramas, getting through the interview, dealing with bitchy colleagues and knowing what to do when your three-year-old screams pathetically as you race off down the garden path, hoping to God the neighbours have been rendered deaf or will decide against tipping off the social services that your child is a prime candidate for the 'at risk' register.

Returning means rapidly rounding the learning curve so that you are not exploited, intimidated or sexually harassed. It means rethinking the running of the house and still having time for sports day and baking cakes for the PTA, and overcoming the disapproval of your mother and husband – who previously never got on, but have become surprisingly chummy over this 'phase' you are going through.

And, uncompromisingly at the top of the Richter scale of items that must be addressed before you even pick up the sits vac column or phone an employment agency, is the question: who is going to not just *mind*, but *care about* the children?

Do not attempt to pass this page if you think that finding a minder will be a doddle, or that you'll cross that bridge when you come to it. Think about it now… because finding the right person to look after your child is a prerequisite to being a working mother.

If it's new technology that's holding you back, then this is the book to reassure you that you are not computer-illiterate, that those terrifyingly intimidating 'explanations' from the technology experts are often no more than a mere ploy to blind you with science, to render you to gibbering insecurity and deeply grateful to yet another expert who can make feeding the cat sound as complicated as performing a frontal lobotomy.

The primary concern of this book is to equip returners with sensible, practical advice and to help them keep a realistic grip on what's ahead. It's a confidence boost for all women who want to return to work full time, who hope to make it a worthwhile part of their life and who see no reason why they shouldn't get back on the career ladder. But it also offers invaluable advice to those who simply want to earn extra money on a part-time basis, those returning after maternity leave and those who are purely interested in voluntary work.

It is also for those who have left a considerably longer gap between child rearing and returning to work and for those looking ahead to the day they, too, might want a change of scenery, once the kids are old enough. And if you are in any doubt when that will be, old enough is that magic age when you are at last able to stand them, but they, for sure, now can't stand you.

A great many women simply want to return to the world of work to widen their social lives, meet new friends and, one mustn't shrink from the fact, there are some who are so turned off by their husband's idea of foreplay that they enter the workplace in search of a brief fling to make them feel alive again, kidding themselves they'll be clever enough to ensure that no-one (ie, their husbands) will be any the wiser. But who am I to tell those of you who want this, that you're more than likely heading for disaster? I will leave that to the very expensive lawyer you will eventually find you are employing to sort out your divorce.

Of course, for anyone so far down the path of needing a little extra-marital activity and to hell with the consequences (because there will be...), there's no doubt they're more likely to achieve this ambition in the workplace than pushing a trolley around Sainsbury's...

If you still feel in need of a shot of courage and are ashamed to admit that re-runs of Dallas at two in the afternoon are fast becoming the highlight of your day, just remember the woman who said: 'Returning to work is a lot easier in the end, than running away from home'.

SECOND TIME AROUND

Chapter One

Someone once defined courage as walking naked through a cannibal village. They were wrong. Courage is deciding to go back to the world of work where, along with daily commuting, new technology, power dressing and being considered 'past it' by the time you're 35, appear to rule.

All this, while your horizons for the past few years have been limited to the school run and Sainsbury's, where your wardrobe has become a powerful tribute to the versatility of the tracksuit, and the only thing that would enhance your favourite dress would be a blackout. Last week you finally mastered the controls on the video. Take heart, I did say *appear* to rule.

'The magazine said dress for success. So I did, plus three inch heels. When I got there, everyone else seemed to be making another kind of fashion statement. Excess is less. I felt like Danny La Rue.'
Jessica, 29, sub editor, Brighton.

'Just in case, I mugged up on everything I could lay my hands on that was proof of youth. I could have reeled off Megadeth's greatest hits, and knew all the best nights at the The Fridge. The youngest person in the office turned out to be 43.'
Marie, 35, insurance clerk, London.

'I thought it would be a miracle if I managed to master the coffee machine and the security system, but by five o'clock on the second day I had cracked the basics of Word Perfect as well. The expensive training school refused to give me a refund.'
Gillian, 30, secretary, Sunderland.

It is a myth, peddled by newspapers and some of the glossy magazines, that the workplace is a high-powered shrine to those men and women who are insensitive to everyone's needs but their own and whose only physical flaws are the blisters gouged on their fingers from crawling up the corporate ladder.

A world where the women are cool, arrogant and ferociously ambitious while managing to be shockingly sexy, as they clinch a multi-million pound deal with men who dress exclusively in Ralph Lauren, look like William Hurt and exchange witty, sophisticated and flirtatiously-loaded conversations over the right brand of coffee: this scenario simply achieves the media's twin ambitions of attracting the right kind of advertising while fuelling the fantasies of some newspaper editors beached on the shores of fantasy.

Admittedly, there are still some who are taken in by the hype, but in reality the workplace these days tends to be full of quite normal people, with mortgages, kids, their mother-in-law arriving like an unstoppable Exocet on Sunday, who shop in Next and Sainsbury's and who dream of going to Tahiti but settle for Tunisia.

They are divorced, single, married, widowed or locked into phoning home three times an hour to check if the middle one's temperature has gone down and the mother's help's spirits have gone up. And the bosses who firmly believe they are God's gift and that you are the chosen recipient.

Working life is full of real people, with real problems, who will never win the pools or be asked to invite *Hello!* into their homes. You will also find a lot of women who took the plunge and went back to work after pausing to have children and those who, for all kinds of reasons, never got around to returning to their jobs straight from maternity leave. Women like you, perhaps?

Work can be the answer to all our prayers (and these days it's got to be some prayer) and it can also be a pain in the butt. It lifts us up, plunges us into despair, brings out the best and the worst in us and can be blamed for everything going wrong in life.

Working life is a curious cocktail of gossip, fact, rumours and ritual. It plays no part in your real life; it's another world where, daily, somewhere between leaving home at eight and returning at whatever hour, you reinvent yourself to become what your job says you are.

It can transform ordinary people into a cast of characters sufficiently fascinating to make soaps redundant and plots more powerful than anything currently found on the best-seller list: the offensively rude boss; the ideas thief; the alcoholic typist; the spaced-out ad director; the office gossip who always gives you the benefit of the dirt; and the boss's mole suffering from acute indiscretion.

Not to mention the Jack-the-lad who comes to work each day from a different direction and the comforting figure of a good mate who wheels you off for a drink when the going gets tough – and together you sip away your troubles while having a good giggle over the office affair that is an open secret.

The number of working women in this country has increased dramatically over the past five or six years. In 1991, 680,000 women returned to full-time employment after bringing up a family and 380,000 returned to part-time work. There were 6,493,000 women with school age children up to 16 years of age, and of these 56.7 per cent were in employment. Of the 3,093,000 women with children up to four years old, a total of 42.6 per cent were working.

Before you start to ask yourself if there is also a place for you beyond the garden gate, you may find it beneficial to answer a few questions in order to discover the simple answer to a more important one…

Remember the time when you said that as soon as the youngest was off to school you'd be going straight back to work? Can you still remember why you said it?

Because you were ambitious and couldn't imagine a life without work, because you wanted to resume a career, because having children was not going to alter your long-term plans and because work was the passport to money, clothes, outings, holidays – and a brilliant career. Well, anyway, a brilliant time without having to give anyone else a thought.

How long ago was all that? Three, five, ten or more years? Like measles and glasses, nothing lasts. Some things change for the better, others for the worse. What you once regarded as a complete bind might now seem totally fascinating. In fact, this could well be the moment to address yourself to what might seem like a silly question: but what, exactly, do you want to get out of work?

If you're looking for equality, fair pay and a world which, after three decades of feminism, must surely have got the message that women count, must not be exploited, must be given the same opportunities, then you will be disappointed. The battle under many guises is far from won.

Not that we are talking here once again about a trip to the barricades, but it must be said that in times of recession, with virtually nothing to protect either a male or female workforce from the most outrageous management exploitation, it would be irresponsible of me not to mention it. More of which later…

Money will of course be a prime motivation for most returners. You need the money. We all do. And because money talks, it also solves complicated arguments at home when you are accused – as you will be – of dereliction of duty.

You might find it reasonable to ally your ambition for a regular four-figure sum in your current account with something that will stimulate your intellect – and possibly in the long run make even more money. Or perhaps you are just sick of being financially dependent on your partner, no matter how supportive he may be.

Of course the real reason for going back to work may well be something quite different; only you know what that is and not every woman wants to work solely for the loot. But let's keep a grip on reality here, money is a very attractive bonus. So if you want to get your hands on some, it is important to make sure that working all the hours God sends is going to produce the results you want.

There's nothing wrong with money. Only in this country do we find it difficult to be seen to want it. In America, for instance, almost the first question asked before you've barely shaken hands is, 'What do you do and how much salary does that carry?' That's not saying it's advisable baldly to announce at an interview that you want to go back to work just for the dosh – in troubled times it helps to have some modicum of interest in the job.

Conversely, missing the stimulation and mental challenge of a job they once trained for is the prime motivation for many other women – who would be willing to work for very little. Women who gave up a good, perhaps well-paid job, for the pleasure of being with their children, who never, for a while at least, considered any other life except that of being a home-maker.

Different ambitions at different times of our lives shape the way we think. There is nothing wrong with feeling it's time to get your own life back into shape before you get too old, too settled, for the challenge of a different routine, new ways of thinking. In fact, before your get-up-and-go has got up and gone.

It is not true that only those women who trained, qualified and successfully practised in their chosen field are the ones who are now champing at the bit to get back to work. Curiously enough, those once high-flyers are often the ones who, having satisfied themselves they could make it on one level, launched themselves wholeheartedly – and with the same enthusiasm – into child rearing and now aren't all that bothered about returning to their former jobs. Which all goes to prove that your background, trained or otherwise, is irrelevant to your current motivation.

There is nothing wrong with admitting that home life is boring you rigid and that, much as you love your children, deeply as you feel for all that matters to them and would never for a second let them think they are less than fascinating, you long to be part of a world that does not regard you simply as an appendage to your family.

There are also a great many loving, devoted, happily married or happily single mothers who want the twin satisfactions of earning money and the chance to beef up their social life.

Finally, there are those who are looking for an affair; who've decided it's time to stop fantasising and to go for the real thing. It is not unknown for the lure of illicit romance to drive a woman to the job centre…

Naturally, one shrinks from intruding on private grief (for that, indeed, is what 99 out of 100 clandestine affairs lead to) but who am I to condemn a woman who daily dreams of romance when she is saddled with the kind of partner who, like a pile of ironing, has to be sorted out once a week – and with marginally less imagination?

So what is your motivation? Money? Companionship? Stimulation? Independence? Or an affair?

Find out by answering the following questions, honestly, and on your own, and without worrying whether you have the 'right approach' to life. This is a private discussion with yourself and not a test. It is to discover what you want out of work, and not to find out if you are the ultimate embodiment of the perfect mother who is returning to the workplace for the 'correct' reasons. There are no correct answers, just truthful ones.

What do you want out of work?

1. Your friends suggest that years at home with the children are taking their toll on your adult personality. Is it because?
a) You don't know the price of a Next blouse but you do know how many cereal box tokens you need to get a Thunderbird figure
b) You know the names of all the *Sesame Street* characters by heart
c) You excuse yourself from the pub bar saying you 'have to go wee-wee'
d) All your sweatshirts have Beatrix Potter characters on them
e) At the last dinner party you absent-mindedly cut up the meat of the man next to you and told him to 'chew nicely'.

2. Your husband's at work, the kids are in school, the house is clean enough and you feel at a loose end. Maybe it's time you went back to work because:
a) If you had a bit of money you could treat yourself to a new outfit or lunch out with your best friend
b) Your best friend is always in a business meeting and can't get away; your second-best friend would have to bring her squally baby along – and you've had enough of those
c) This morning you realised you were concentrating hard on reading the back of the cornflake packet and finding it interesting
d) The teachers, children at school, your neighbours, refer to you as 'Tristan's mother' and don't know your first name even though you've lived in the same house for five years
e) You haven't felt sexy since the last time the window cleaner smiled at you through the curtains.

3. A friend has just started as a volunteer dogsbody for a children's charity. Your first reaction is:
a) She's mad to do all that work and not get paid for it
b) It's no better than being at home: she'll be talking to children half the day
c) I suppose it's a worthwhile cause and something different
d) I couldn't stand being ordered about by all those Lady Bountifuls in charge
e) No point in buying a new wardrobe: it's all women and children.

4. You know you will have to start at the bottom of the ladder but you still daydream about being company chairman one day because then you could:
a) Quadruple your salary and find out what luxury really means
b) Gather together a management team of razor-sharp, ambitious women and build an empire
c) Never again be bored in your life
d) Run your life, and everyone else's, your own way: power is very liberating
e) Order that new junior manager to be stripped, washed... and brought to the executive suite.

5. At a school reunion, the most successful, high-powered careerist of your year is holding the table enthralled with her tales of globe-trotting wheeling and dealing. What impresses you most is the fact that:
a) Her wardrobe allowance is equal to your mortgage
b) She has friends, dry-cleaners, store credit cards and a car mechanic in every European capital
c) She blooms on three hours sleep a night because the days are so fascinating
d) She never calls home
e) She had to learn French, Spanish, Italian, Swedish and German to communicate with the men in her life – and not by taking off her clothes.

6. A girlfriend suggests you treat yourselves to a weekend at a health spa. You agree because:
a) It's a good investment, physically and mentally
b) You might meet a few recuperating TV personalities
c) It's located in spectacular countryside and the fresh air and scenery will be invigorating
d) No-one will be able to interrupt you when you're settled with a novel... or want another drink of water after lights out or need a fairy costume made overnight for the school play
e) You'll be primed for the first lovely man you meet afterwards.

7. Your husband rails at the idea of working women because half the women in his office, he says, are having affairs with their co-workers. Does this:

a) Exasperate you: most of them are there to pay the bills
b) Make you understand why, if they all have husbands like yours
c) Make you rethink your working wardrobe and shorten your skirts in hope
d) Make you angry: it sounds like an excuse to keep women out of the workforce
e) Shock you… what, only half?

8. The best part of the working week must be:
a) Pay day
b) Lunchtime when you gossip with your mates
c) The morning ideas meeting where the arguments flow thick and fast
d) Seeing the children off to school, waving your partner goodbye, closing the door on last night's pizza, the laundry, the dog hair and the wall of crayon art… and setting off for a new day
e) When the Kevin Costner lookalike brings around the mail.

9. You and your partner have a furious row, the children are whining that everything's boring and your mother-in-law says she's coming for the weekend. Do you wish you could rush off to work:
a) Thinking that on your salary you could just afford a one-way ticket to Rio and forget about the lot of them
b) Then you would only have to contain yourself until you met a friend at the coffee machine to whom you can let off steam
c) So you can shove it all to the back of your mind and concentrate on sorting out the company's problems – surely a soothing exercise?
d) Knowing that at work at least things are orderly and unruffled and domestic issues have no importance
e) Because you could ring that chap in accounts payable and take him up on his offer for lunch.

10. A delicious Harrison Ford-type is waiting for you to join the company and no-one could possibly fail to notice the quivering tension between you. Do you think:
a) I would resist him. Now that Sophie's got a brace on her teeth and Lucy's started piano lessons and we've added that conservatory, it's not worth the hassle of losing a job

b) He'll be nothing but trouble, the whole department would be fighting over him

c) It makes work interesting. I could always say 'yes' to lunch and dinner but 'no' to breakfast

d) He would be used to women feeding out of his hand, why should I add to his ego?

e) I could always dash out at lunchtime and get my legs waxed and buy some La Perla underwear.

How did you score?

Mostly a's: Money is the main motivation for your return to the workplace and, as long as you think you're being decently paid, you'll put in the hours and put up with the occasional slings and arrows of working life.

Mostly b's: The big lure of work for you is the companionship of your colleagues and the feeling of being part of the office community. Every workplace is like a small village: there are heroes and villains, gossips, the hard-done-by, the mysterious; being an 'insider' and a sense of belonging is very important to you.

Mostly c's: Does ICI know you're available? You look to a job for stimulation and thrive on the parry and thrust of office life, politics and all. You're not afraid of the bad times – the unpredictability and changes in working life are what make it interesting.

Mostly d's: Okay, work beckons. But you've got to stop watching re-runs of *The Hand That Rocks The Cradle*. Working helps you hang on to your sense of identity and work is the place where you are judged by your performance, not for being someone's wife, mother, daughter. It gives you self-respect and assurance.

Mostly e's: Yes, you're ready all right – for an affair. There are worse reasons for going to work in the hope of meeting Mr Wonderful (or even Mr Okay For The Afternoon) but you should be aware of the pitfalls. Office romances rarely remain secret and being the butt of gossip is never pleasant. Bosses may take a dim view too (unless they're involved) so you have to weigh up carefully what's at risk and – is it worth it?

If you think that's settled that, that you now know it's the money you want, or the freedom or the independence, pause for a moment. Is returning to work going to meet those aims?

Take money for instance. Not many of us stuck for a quid or the mortgage has much choice in the matter, but you really should, as far as possible, adopt a short term plan allied to your financial situation. This isn't a luxury decision exclusively catering for those who have the choice. It's a real, hard, immovable fact, that unless you have sorted out what the money is for – paying off debts, school fees, a holiday, car, whatever – you can end up whacked out, bored silly and still have very little to show for it.

'The mortgage was crippling, so I rang an ad in the local paper looking for people to sell space. I then had this enormous phone bill which they assessed on the basis of how much space I had sold, and it was hopeless.'
Winnie, 34, Enfield.

'They said with tips I could make about two hundred quid a week, but I couldn't do evenings, just lunches, and it was very quiet. I was earning a pittance.'
Sally, 29, Penzance.

'The job was an hour's journey and in a part of town where the nearest shops were ten minutes away by bus. I started using expensive time-savers: taxis, takeaways, that kind of thing. Really, I should have asked for more money in the first place. It was just that I was so grateful I'd got a job.'
Geraldine, 36, Milton Keynes.

Even if the money is great, what is the point of getting a job that pays a fortune but has all the mental stimulation to be found on the production line of the Smethwick Ball Bearing Factory when you were looking for a challenge?

Women re-entering the job market at a time when good jobs, *any* jobs, are at a premium, may well find that for all the fine talk as we turned the decade about working mothers being the hope for the future, in truth are not going to be spoilt for choice.

'What did I miss most when I left the factory? The money, of course, but I missed my mind even more while I was there.'
Jackie, 33, lab technician, Birmingham.

'Never take a job, if you're looking for companionship, that says "small friendly office". That's you, two happily married quantity surveyors and a bored junior who thinks you're as old as Noah. When all I wanted was to meet someone to go to the next Paul Simon concert with. All right the Chippendales, if you insist.'
Myra, 41, catering manager, Sutton.

Not getting the job you really want doesn't mean you shouldn't direct your energies to where you are most likely to satisfy your ambition. Dream on... Even if you take any job to get you back into the job market – enough to make that psychological jump from home to office – don't give up on *why* you want to go back, just keep looking for the answer.
If you are desperate for a challenge, what is the point of taking a job where all the decisions are made by eight Generals? The position of 'adaptable assistant to five young dynamic sales execs' is not for you. (That's unless you're looking for an affair – one of them is bound to be playing away from home if national statistics are anything to go by.) And neither is the company wanting 'someone imbued with team spirit'. No, no, this is just another General looking for more Indians to order around. But if, on the other hand, you're looking for companionship, a laugh and a lunchtime drink at the wine bar, go for it. Leave the corporate decisions to the chiefs, that's what they're paid for.

'In the end I started to think laterally. Where would I meet the most people? And then, what could I do in that company? I applied for and got a job as a trainee sales assistant in the town's department store.'
Gemima, 31, sales supervisor, Bangor.

If it's a challenge you want, far better to take a closer look at 'enterprising person willing to take responsibility for setting up new department'. Even if the money is peanuts (and surely someone as enterprising as you can change all that?) you will never again find yourself discussing Maastricht with anyone, let alone your five-year-old. Working mothers don't have time for idle gossip.

ALL IN THE FAMILY – AND LET'S KEEP IT THAT WAY
Chapter Two

I f you want the pleasure of watching your entire family revealing their skills as emotional vampires, try telling them you are going back to work. There is plenty of proof in every street in the land that most husbands and children regard the needs of a wife and mother as something to be indulged only after everyone else's needs have been met. However, you may be surprised to find that you have fewer problems with the children than with your partner.

Let it be said at once that I personally know not just a few, but many, dads who care wonderfully for their children, who do not see having to do the housework, cooking and shopping, on top of their own job, as any big deal. In fact, some men now claim that women are learning to cook and iron just in case they *don't* get married.

There is no scientific evidence to back this up, but it seems to me, looking around my own friends and relatives, that the men who feel most at ease in this role are the ones who grew up with sisters, working mothers (in whatever capacity) or who genuinely really like women.

But they are still in the minority. Far too many husbands and partners still feel threatened by the whole notion of working mothers and just take it for granted that even in these liberated times you wouldn't dream of allowing such a thought to enter your head.

There are those convinced you are already looking for an affair and others who feel haunted by the thought that you might bring home a bigger wage than *his* (chance would be a fine thing). There are those who treat your decision to return as punishable only by periods of long silences, even less co-operation around the house than you already get, and who thereafter pursue a constant quest for evidence of how selfish and damaging your decision is.

'We don't talk any more,' they will say on day two of your new working life, when, finally, after ten years of being the one who listened, you too can contribute to the dinner table conversation about

'What I did at the office today'.

'You're so different since you started that job. I don't know, not as *warm* as you used to be.' This when you ask him to massage *your* feet for once after you've been standing most of the day at the shop.

'Funny,' they have been known to say, as they fork the first takeaway they've had in a month around their plate, 'how fast fast food becomes part of your life.'

'Children of working mothers never do as well as those with a stay-at-home-mum,' he might say, when your eleven-year-old gets a B– for an essay (which as usual you wrote for him), instead of his customary B+. Male insecurity parades itself in these times in a way that would keep all 127 psychological schools of thought on behaviour patterns occupied for a year.

Far too many women report their other half's reaction to the news that they are considering returning to work as, 'Great… as long as it doesn't affect the kids'. Whatever happened to New Man? He who claims he thinks about his partner's feelings, wants her to be equal, agrees she must have a life of her own and independence?

He will be quick to conjure up a vision of himself and the children huddled together in a cold, cheerless kitchen, surrounded by empty cupboards, the youngest asking pitifully, 'When's Mummy coming home, Daddy?' He will also be convinced that you are planning to run off with the chief cashier who has been doling out your expenses and much else besides.

It's at this point that you understand that while few women admit their age, few men act theirs, and what you have possibly done to stir such a fertile imagination is beyond guessing. Marriages were a battlefield of wills long before the working mother. 'I was thinking about taking a job' is the killer line. But it shouldn't be. Nor should you be intimidated by it.

If the mortgage has become a living nightmare, the car is about to be repossessed, your ex has stopped paying maintenance and can't be found by your lawyer to discuss why not, or you have just bought a coat from Oxfam which *you* gave *them* a year ago, I see no reason why your most beloved shouldn't understand your reasons for returning to work. And if those reasons include a decent holiday, a few guilt-free lunches with your friends, a night out without raiding the family allowance, it all sounds perfectly reasonable to me.

Unfortunately, after years of putting everyone else's needs before their own, most women find trying to explain that all they want is a bit of freedom and a few luxuries begins to sound about as reasonable as announcing they are going on the game.

'But why? What's the matter? It's that bloody best friend of yours isn't it, putting ideas into your head.'
Mary's husband, Jon, surveyor, Huddersfield.

'I don't mind. As long as you're still here for the children when they come in. That's right, isn't it kids?'
Marian's husband, Simon, accountant, Wallsall.

'Oh, I see. You want me to increase the housekeeping? Well, just say so, I hate blackmail.'
Vannessa's husband, Mark, company secretary, Stirling.

'You what…? Don't be stupid. You've got enough to do.'
Sarah's husband, Robert, insurance salesman, Oxford.

'He said, "When I married you, you didn't have a rag on your back" and I said, "No, but I've got plenty now". What's *wrong* with wanting to buy some clothes for *me*?'
Janet, husband Paul, accounts clerk, Torbay.

These are almost better responses than the ones who play the martyr/portray you as selfishly unreasonable/assume your relationship is under threat. ('I see, I'm not doing enough for you, is that it? After all I've done. Do you think I *like* working for that bloody company. Don't you think I would like to just sit at home spending the money instead of earning it?') And all you want to do, for heaven's sake, is *work*.
In spite of what everyone tells you about being your own woman, you'll find that asserting your rights, standing firm, isn't easy in practice.
And as for all those self-growth books with titles like 'You Too Are A Real Person', 'How To Be True To Yourself', 'Why You Must be Selfish To Survive', I swear each and every one was written by

someone who has never had to face the kind of moral outrage women generally confront when they tell their partner and/or children that the live-in house slave is breaking free.

Some women, unfortunately, in the build-up to the confrontation, have argued the case so long and so exhaustingly in their own heads that they're in danger of losing the first round. In mentally compiling their argument for the return, they've cranked themselves up to a high pitch of resentment about the unfairness of it all – add to that overwhelming guilt for even daring to *think* it and, in the end, what was supposed to be a calm announcement, turns into such a bitter catalogue of accusations and reproaches that the entire family, not to mention their primary relationship, is pushed on to completely new ground.

If, however, you have the kind of partner who supports your decision wholeheartedly and doesn't have to be reminded that his share of the workload on the home front will increase… well terrific.

Even so, whatever your real reason for returning to work (as established in chapter one) my advice is to keep it to yourself – and just to say that you're doing it for the money. It's so much easier to say you want them to share in your new-found financial status than to explain that: home life is boring you witless; you yearn to have your own bank account; as fiercely as you love them you now need to bring something other than *their* worries and concerns to the dinner table. I think you'll find that money talks…

… a longed-for holiday, cash to pay off the car, some new trainers, a video machine or Sega's Game Gear plus Sonic Hedgehog 2. Whatever it takes, throw it in. Although I am all for talking things through with your partner and children, I am not averse to a little bribery. (It also assuages guilt…)

Life is too short for discussions on the level of 'You are parading all the chauvinistic sexual politics that spawned separatist feminism', or that degenerate into 'Because I want to…' or 'It's not fair…' And please, I beg of you, never *ask* whether you can return to work, or cajole or plead to do so. You do not have to ask permission for anything once you are over 18. If you seriously believe you have to ask permission, then I seriously think you need to re-draw the ground rules for your relationship. It all sounds very one-sided to me.

On the other hand, I don't think it's a good idea to simply march out of the house and off to work, having been the central figure in their lives for the past decade. After all, how would you feel if your husband came home one night and suddenly announced that he had just jacked his job in? You might well back him every inch of the way, but you would have liked, at least, to have known how he felt about his job and been included in his plans, wouldn't you?

But what if you're a single mother or newly divorced, the maintenance is a long time coming and/or you know if you don't get out of the house you are going to go off your rocker?

In a funny kind of way, your children will probably be far more receptive and tolerant of your decision to go to work (even relieved if it guarantees to cheer you up, and stops you focusing on their every move), but if they have had the trauma of a separation from their father, or any other difficult experience, take it easy, as much for your own sake as theirs.

However, children are surprisingly tolerant of adult decisions and usually very adaptable to change, provided they are put in the picture and are totally reassured they won't be too affected. What they want to know is, exactly who will be there when they get in from school, or meet them at the school gates? Who is going to get them tea and take them to Brownies, cubs, around to Mark's or Sally's?

If they know exactly where to find you, should they need you, they'll be happy. If you are going out for your company on business calls, leave instructions with your office to let your children know where you can be reached. And make absolutely sure the school has an up-to-date phone number and contact name where they can get you at any time.

If they know they can phone you at the office the minute they get in just to say, 'Hi, we're back' (and any company that frowns on that, tell them to stuff their job), and to have a quick conversation, this will stave off a lot of problems. They just need to tell you that their teacher was rotten to them, they need help with their homework, can they go to Johnny's party. Even the best home-help in the world shouldn't be allowed to eclipse this. If you're not available when they call, make sure your secretary or someone in the office can pass a message on, to say you will call back directly.

Do not feel guilty or panic stricken. Get into the habit of calling this couple of minutes, list time. All the things to be discussed once you get back. And stick to it. Most children, once they have unloaded the problem (which might seem trivial to everyone else, but is world-shattering to them) are much happier.

The point is you must be get-attable reasonably quickly. But don't become paranoic; just remember that when you were at home, there were times when you went out shopping, and so on, which meant a temporary blackout in communication.

If you can take home the occasional treat, in the eyes of your children this will help shed some light – and sense – on your working life. On one occasion during my first week back at work (my children were aged nine and 12) I nearly kicked an acquaintance on a crowded train for looking disapprovingly at my WH Smith bag of goodies. 'They'll expect you to do it every week,' she warned. They didn't, but so what if they had?

Many children of working mothers do get a bit spoiled, but the vast majority grow up to be very nice and well-balanced, and the most anti-social they'll get is arguing about what time they'll be in, assuming that money grows on trees, growing their hair too long, answering you back, falling in love with the wrong person, violently disagreeing with everything you say or do and always being ready to give you the benefit of their inexperience.

The children of non-working mothers do much the same.

Anti-social behaviour is not the sole result of working mothers, single mothers or any other mother. There is not one scrap of evidence, any report or government commission to prove it.

Such evidence might well show that some children who abscond from home or school, who are unable to read or write by the time they are 15 and who mug people in the streets, do have working mothers. But believe me, they usually have quite a few more problems to cope with beyond having a mother who happens to go to work: things such as a father they never see or who doesn't give a damn about them, poor diet, inadequate housing. These children would benefit from better provision for after-school care, tougher legislation on making absent fathers pay up and stronger support for single mothers – of whom 70 per cent in Britain live on or below the poverty line.

All of which has nothing to do with those neglectful, irresponsible women who should not be left in charge of the family cat. The two are often lumped together to prove a point and it is dangerous, misleading and insulting to the thousands of single, working mothers who daily work hard to keep their families together (and the vast majority do) and make all kinds of personal sacrifices in doing so.

It is important not to allow such reporting to determine arguments about why you should not go to work; especially if you live in a nice neighbourhood, your children go to half-way decent schools and, as far as you know, your husband/partner has a job and is not on Interpol's wanted list.

In fact, since childcare is at the centre of feminist concerns, campaigning vigorously and vocally for improved childcare facilities, it simply doesn't add up that the feminists are the same women who 'abandon' their children on the altar of their own selfish ambitions.

A friend once said she thought all this emphasis on deprivation and separation said to be inflicted on children of working mothers was no more than a male plot to keep women in a jelly-like state of guilt and therefore easier to manipulate. Occasionally, just occasionally, I believe her. For instance, if you have a partner who uses the children to control what you do, you might recognise the following scenario:

Your new company think you've got what it takes and arranges to send you on a management training course which involves an overnight stay. You go and do well. Three months later they want you to represent them at a weekend conference.

He says: 'Listen, Mum's company are sending her to a conference for the weekend – how should I know what it's about? Learning how to rule the world, I expect. She'll be gone longer than she was before, do you mind?'

Since when you went away last time they were left with a brooding, irritable father to care for them, it's no surprise that the children protest. Not because they don't want their mother to go, but because they don't want to be left with bootfaced Dad.

No-one denies that separation anxiety is very real to children, but today it is equally known that short term separation causes little or no such anxiety if the parent/relative/friend left in charge is just as loving and caring. In fact, approached sensibly, the change for a child can be an enjoyable experience.

Mobilising guilt in a working mother is easier than drawing breath and it does no working mother, whether new to the game or a seasoned campaigner, any harm to learn to recognise guilt-inducers when they see them.

The partner really worth making sacrifices for, however, is the one who says: 'Listen, great news. Mum's boss thinks she's brilliant – but we could have told him that, couldn't we? So while she's away let's sort out the Christmas decorations/watch that video she hates/each invite a friend for Saturday lunch/visit granny/take a boat ride/stay up late…'

Before telling your family you're serious about work, devise a plan about the way the house will be organised from now on, taking into account their routines and timetables. If, over the years, you've allowed it to become fact that everyone in your house is incapable of operating any piece of machinery unless it's the television, video, Nintendo or computer, now's the time to introduce them to the wonders of kitchen technology.

This business of getting the family to help out, does not, I must warn you, come easily to most women. Organising everything from shopping to making the fairy costume for the school play is a role they will not want to relinquish easily. There is also a deep fear that the family they have nurtured and cared for all those years is now incapable of doing the smallest thing for themselves.

However, think this through: if your 14-year-old son (even your 12-year-old) is capable of playing rugby/soccer/cricket/baseball with the tenacity of a man auditioning for the SAS, I think we can assume he is strong enough to carry back the videos and collect the dry cleaning.

Any daughter (aged ten and over) who spends hours locked in the bathroom and emerges smelling like a direct hit on a perfume factory, can clean the bath.

If Dad is capable of controlling the buying for BigStocks Incorporated, he can crack the weekly/monthly shopping for a family of four.

If you approach all this with the sensitivity of an over-excited sergeant major, you will, of course, get an equally agitated, even mutinous response. Point out that by them pitching in, you will still have time when you get home to drive them to the cinema, round to their friends, even take them out somewhere special.

Don't believe all those articles that insist you should just *make* them do the household chores; partly because it won't work all the time, and partly because to minimise your guilt you still need to feel a central part of their lives. Try asking for help calmly. Make it all sound simple and, if you can afford it, simplify your life: a washing machine, dryer, and a cleaning lady once a week if you can.

No-one irons sheets or underwear these days, so stop it if you do. Self-defrosting fridges and self-cleaning ovens are a boon – and learn to shut the door on children's bedrooms that look like the aftermath of a burglary. Have days when all library books and videos must go back. Assign days for football shirts to get washed and mended, when hems are taken up, shirt buttons replaced.

Partners should be praised for their contribution. If you have allowed them to believe that you are solely responsible for the domestic side of life, you really cannot expect to hit them with accusations of chauvinism and sexism out of the blue simply because it no longer fits in with your plans.

Above all, don't get so wrapped up in your new job that it starts to come before your family. Precious family units of the kind we have been discussing do not last forever – children grow up, go away – and are not to be sacrificed to *any* job. It sounds a bit corny, I know, but time alone with your partner is paramount. You should try to spend at least one evening a week together, away from the children, relaxing and talking over what you've been up to, arguing about your friends, deciding where to go on holiday.

The truth is that, one year on, most husbands can be heard reluctantly admitting that since you started work, you have become livelier, younger, more interesting… and neither do marriages crack up because women go back to work – if they do, they were in a rough state to start with, so don't blame work.

It is true, too, that working women have affairs. But then the opportunity to do so has increased and, if lack of opportunity was all that prevented this from happening before, then again it sounds as if the relationship was heading for trouble anyway.

The ground rule for introducing a new element into the lives of your nearest and dearest – and after all that's all going back to work is – is to make sure that each and every one of them realises you are not putting work before them. And all that means is a bit more reassuring and a few more hugs all round.

On the other hand, do not try to alleviate your husband's feelings of insecurity by pinning his work up alongside the kids' paintings on the fridge door.

WHAT GOES OUT MUST COME IN
Chapter Three

I f you think you're over the hurdle on the home front and have established exactly why you want to return to work – whether for money, freedom or independence – pause for a moment. What, if by going back to work in order to solve those problems, you'll just be replacing them with others?

Take money for instance. Not many of us stuck for enough to make ends meet has much choice in the matter, but you really should adopt, as far as possible, a realistic working plan allied to a serious consideration about your finances. That means not only making sure working isn't going to cost you, but also warding off a possible bit of manipulation because you look and sound vulnerable to a prospective employer.

Don't assume that all employers are just lying in wait for the weak link in society to come knocking on their door. Most of them are decent, straightforward and just looking for results, not scoring points. But what good will knowing that do for you, if you don't learn to recognise the ones out to make a fast buck at your expense?

If you want to earn money for a specific reason, then make sure that working all the hours God sends is definitely going to produce the results you want. Surprisingly, the cost of going to work can add up to more than staying at home. The cost of childcare alone is daunting, especially if you're a single parent. But even in a committed, supportive relationship it can still seem about as hefty as the national debt.

Personally, I don't believe that the salary of the nanny or childminder should be seen as exclusively your responsibility. If your husband or partner is going to benefit financially and emotionally by you working (even if at first he doesn't appreciate the fact) then he should fork out at least half the cost of having his children cared for. Any man who says, 'It's your choice, so you pay', and then happily and silently benefits from all the extras, is a schmuck. And you are a very nice person to allow him to do so – but an assertiveness training course would soon help you see the money being more wisely spent and you being taken less for granted.

And then there are your working clothes to think about. Unless you're going to be provided with some kind of uniform, you will have to buy at least two or three decent outfits to see you through the working week.

'I've got a dress for every day of the week, and this is it.'
Polly, 37, High Wycombe.

'This is my religious dress, because every time I wear it my husband says, "Oh God".'
Jenny, 44, South Shields.

On top of that you will have to count makeup, fares, lunch out (unless you take a packed lunch which means another task each day) and a wild dash around Tesco after work which will push up the shopping bill. Fast food, pre-cooked meals, treats to bribe the kids, your own guilt, do not come cheap.

On the other hand, as long as working doesn't cost you any *more* than staying at home, if on balance your sanity and confidence are being kept intact and if you also regard it as an investment for the future then, even if you only break even, it is worth it.

But starting out by owing money, and then finding you owe more, is clearly not.

Do not despair. Do not even groan at the next bit. Believe me, there are more ways of solving the misery of being trapped between four walls with the school run and the supermarket marking your horizons without actually 'going to work'.

Voluntary work won't earn you money, but it will push the fringes of your life a bit further out, broaden your contacts locally, make you feel involved – and you wouldn't believe how satisfying it can be to raise money for charity, keep the school on its toes by joining the PTA, help the elderly or lend a hand at the local hospital, charity shop or car boot sale.

In times of recession, many men and women turn to voluntary work for a number of reasons; mostly to keep them involved and to retain a sense of doing something useful with their lives.

Mary Tucker, a senior counsellor with the Citizens Advice Bureaux in London, is one who encourages women to take up voluntary work. 'It is socially valuable, intellectually stimulating and can provide volunteers with opportunities to do a wide range of work with responsibilities far wider than they would get in paid employment,' she explains. 'Voluntary work can be an introduction to the discipline of the workplace.

'Mothers are used to being the ones who fetch and carry for the family, including pets, grandparents and neighbours. Their time is not valued by anyone, including themselves. When they become a volunteer they become part of a team, they need to be at work when they say they will. It can be the beginning of an outside life in gradual stages.'

Charity work does not necessarily mean solemn, intense people who take Life Very Seriously. Responsibly, yes. And indeed you do get some organisers who have misunderstood their role and make the average Field Marshall sound reasonable and, yes, you do come across some middle-class women who could teach a Calcutta beggar a thing or two about extracting money from unsuspecting passers-by, but there are not many like that.

Curiously enough, it is those avenues often dismissed as simply platforms for bored mothers, local do-gooders and those who didn't manage to avoid the vicar in the high street when he was casting around for helpers for the bazaar, that are fertile ground for networking, know what jobs are going locally, will help you with your own problems and generally boost your morale.

'Afterwards a crowd of us went to the pub and ended up planning for us all to go on a day trip to France. It wasn't what I expected. But then I never thought I would agree to joining a fund raising day for a school library.'
Heather, 39, Preston.

'The vicar wanted some mothers to help organise the school choir for a carol concert. I ended up singing in a local choir and I've never met so many people, or travelled so much since.'
Mary, 35, Cheam, Surrey.

And on the same subject – morale that is – enroling for a course in anything that interests you at the local adult education centre will get you out of the house, improve your qualifications (even if you don't take any exams) and won't cost much either.

'I was so depressed that in the end my best friend dragged me along to a course she was doing in domestic science. I sulked all the way there, refused to smile at the lecturer's jokes and marvelled at the number of bored women who made up the class. These days I take one of the classes myself.'
Sandy, 47, Fleetwood.

'Pure chance really. A friend asked if I could cover for her at the hospital shop just for a week while she had a holiday. While I was there I saw a poster about training to be a counsellor. It's the most satisfying job I've ever had – especially as I work from home.'
Rosemary, 41, Walsall.

You may not be that lucky. But think about it? What have you got to lose, especially if paid employment isn't immediately going to solve your problems or you can't instantly find a job? And it doesn't half help to puff up your CV when you're firing it off to prospective employers.

The only way you will know which is better for you is to do a spot of assessing. Discover what the current rate for the job you're looking for is likely to be and take into account how this will affect tax, maintenance and child support. At the time of writing, you are entitled to a personal allowance before paying tax of £3,445 a year and, if you are a one parent family, you can claim an additional allowance for your first child.

Choosing the right pension plan, investments and so on? This is the time to introduce yourself to the bank manager, but they're always getting a bad press so don't expect too much of a welcome. And remember… once they give you an overdraft you are forever in their debt. Come to think of it, don't expect an apology when they get things wrong, on no account expect an efficient service, and regard it as a bonus if they remember who you are and actually treat you as someone who can add up.

Please don't take your troubles to a financial adviser. You will only end up with a dozen pension plans you don't need – they are just salesmen after all.

This is a good time to recall why you wanted a job so much. Because you couldn't get yourself a drink of water without fetching drinks for two or three others at the same time. And you'd run out of permutations of how to wear a tracksuit...

Meanwhile, how can you tell if it's worth all the hassle? Because everyone's circumstances varies, it would be impossible in the space of this book to work out exactly who would and who wouldn't benefit by working.

For example, if you are married and your husband works, and your joint salaries will cover the extra expense of child-minding, you may well benefit financially from getting a job.

But if you're a single mother with two children living in rented accommodation and relying on Income Support as well as maintenance from the children's father, then you might find that taking a job that pays more than the basic non-taxable wage will automatically lose you your Income Support. (It might also come to the ears of your former partner that you are earning money and signal his arrival at the solicitor's office, pressing for a reduction in the already paltry financial contribution he makes to his children's lives.) If your husband is made redundant and you have three children, but you are capable of earning above the national average and land a job that pays this, you won't be entitled to any Income Support until his redundancy money starts running out or disappears altogether. And remember, no family can get Income Support if one partner is working more than 16 hours a week.

Single mothers are the most vulnerable and there's no way anyone can dispute that. They are the ones jostling to get out of the poverty trap, only to find that whenever they try to climb out someone pushes the ladder away.

There are still some lunatic politicians who continue to insist that single mothers are at the root of society's ills, when all too often all they are denied is the luxury of minimum choice. It is not single parents who cause social problems, it is the way we treat them in the first place that creates the problem.

If you are a lone parent wanting to get back to work and need specific financial advice, I urge you to contact Gingerbread (071 240 0953) or the National Council for One Parent Families (071 267 1361), either of whom will put you in touch with the right people. If you are getting benefit, check how much you need to earn to be better off working.

Don't listen to what your friend who has gone back tells you, or the woman next door, or the girl behind the counter. You are an individual and your circumstances – and your spirit – are going to be different from theirs. What to them is an insurmountable problem, you might take in your stride; what they consider a cinch could give you pause for thought.

Assuming that you have worked out the finances and decided that it is worth going back to work, be warned: never take less than the going rate for the job.

Something like twelve and a half thousand jobs have been created for women in the last two years. Such work is in the main part-time, and while this is sometimes better than nothing, it also means it's twice as likely that no man responsible for a family could afford to take on the jobs that have been created, on the salary offered. So don't be lured into believing that you are being paid a reasonable amount without checking what similar jobs are paying.

When companies are cutting back, managements are nearly always utterly ruthless about exploiting insecurity. It is now common to hear of managers who grudgingly pay their staff a minumum salary, expect them to do the job of two, even three, and also push the number of working hours to, and over, the limit.

Hysterical outbursts when the workforce protest that they are already doing more than anyone could expect for the money and time being invested, coupled with an astonishment that the said workforce does not feel inclined to hover near exhaustion point for the sole benefit of the MD's personal bank balance, is unhappily the norm. Even more common is the blunt response, 'Don't do it then, I'll get someone else who will'. And sadly they can.

There is a widely held, but utterly misplaced, belief on the part of some managements that the workforce is in total ignorance of the economy and unable to read a balance sheet. This is sold under phrases like, 'I'm afraid the days are gone when we could pay overtime/afford a secretary/invest in decent surroundings (except for my office which is for visitors, as you know)'. Or, 'There are queues of people waiting to take your job/no other company is paying more/Bloggs Brothers are getting results with half the staff'.

Most workforces can work out what the company is spending and on what, and the sad facts of a bungled balance sheet are not hard to read.

There is no doubt that companies, old and new, use a weak economic climate to exploit men and women – especially women – who arc in no position to negotiate all that strongly.

All this is crude and vulgar and, sadly, statistically unprovable, although Mary Tucker is inclined to say, 'I wonder…' And even more sadly, few people feel strong enough, or have the resources, to risk challenging these claims.

If you have nothing to lose, do not be deterred by these arguments. Charity does not exist. If they think you are good enough to do the job, then you are good enough to be paid properly.

Most companies, if you remain polite, courteous and firm, will squeeze a little more out of the budget (while urging you not to tell any of the other employees). However, it is only worth pushing if you have done your homework and know for a stone cold certain fact that elsewhere the rate is higher… and you can risk being turned down.

Remember. Is going back to work going to cost you more than staying at home? If so, then it isn't worth crossing your fingers and hoping that you can improve the situation once you start the job. You won't.

Exploitation takes many forms but none so blatant as those of women returning to work after a baby. It's worth mentioning here that it is not always the employer's fault if things go wrong – but it nearly always is.

The biggest problem confronting any woman who confidently expects to resume the role she left after she returns from maternity leave is that her replacement doesn't want to relinquish the reins or the company have now decided – without any evidence other than their own prejudice – that the returner is not going to be so committed.

Astonishing though this may seem, women employers who should know better are among the offenders. And fresh from maternity leave is not the best time to be taking on the boss, male or female: emotionally there are very few woman who find it easy to leave a very young baby and return to work, and in that frame of mind the chances of your winning your job back are severely reduced.

The saddest fact is that the number of mothers returning to work after the birth of a baby only to face demotion or the sack is actually on the increase. Again, the recession is blamed or the company have 'misunderstood' the mother's intentions. Rubbish.

It would, of course, be wonderful if you could quietly and peacefully blank your mind to everything but having your child. But, frankly, you cannot legislate for what goes on in anyone's mind and maternity leave is still regarded as an interruption most companies would prefer not to have.

The fact that a male executive might well have a heart attack (from too many business lunches, being chauffeur-driven everywhere and the strain of an office affair) and be absent for six months, doesn't seem to amount to the same thing. At least a pregnant woman gives the company seven months notice of her intended absence, not seven minutes.

The best advice I can give you is this: if you genuinely want to return to your job, then stay in touch with the office, continue to check reports, ask for updates, remain part of the decision-making process if that is your role. The contact must not be via a junior colleague but through the head of your department and, if necessary, send the MD copies of any memos you write.

Even if you don't physically appear at the office, it is then impossible for them to sustain any credible defence which says they misunderstood your intentions. Women who disappear completely for 29 weeks while they give birth and adjust to the new member of the family, and who make no attempt to even call the office until they are nearly ready to go back, should not be surprised when the management display doubts about their commitment.

Of course, this in no way justifies handing over your job to someone else or offering you something that is nowhere near as senior as the job you left, but you will have a harder task proving your dedication. After all, seven months is a long time to stay silent. Office life can change in days, and your presence will soon be a distant memory if you don't make it felt.

By far the best approach is to establish your position before taking your leave. Get it in writing that you will be returning to the same job, at the same salary (plus any company increases that might have taken place), and that you expect to be kept up to date with your work during your absence.

What about if you have your baby, fully intending to go back to work, and then find that your feelings about working have changed? The idea of promoting the wonders of TopDog International suddenly palls beside the fascinating daily discoveries of what your heir or heiress can do, and you don't want to miss a moment.

Be reasonable. Let the company know as soon as you can. Then perhaps you could even negotiate some continued link, maybe work part time, from home. Who knows, you may need them in a couple of years.

And if you do go back only to find it isn't working out, that you are too tired, too distracted, to work efficiently, make sure you have given yourself enough time to judge whether *you* want to pack it in, move to a slower track, or tough it out.

Curiously enough, it can be easier to negotiate for a job, coming from a long career break, than to find yourself on the sharp end of a company who wants your job for someone else within weeks of temporarily vacating the chair on maternity leave. Very often you will find that while you have still got the same title, your duties will have changed. The person doing 'your' job has fitted in and you have to negotiate equivalent duties.

However, in all cases, never assume you can work everything out once you get there. You can't. It may all sound more trouble than it's worth (well, sometimes it is) but most of the time it isn't, which – in case you're beginning to wonder – is why I'm writing this book.

Anyone can write about the good times, but it wouldn't be fair to say working life is easy. It can be, but only if you know your way around it.

MOTHER'S LITTLE HELPER – AND DAD'S

Chapter Four

'**M**andy seemed so nice, and the children liked her, so I hired her. After a month, another mother asked me if I knew that Sam, my eight-year-old, was walking home from school on his own. Mandy said she thought he was old enough. I said I thought she should get another job.'
Sarah, 34, architect, Swansea.

'On the way to work, I saw a newspaper with the screaming headline, "Child disappears while nanny entertained boyfriend". I got off the bus, took a taxi all the way back home and resigned the following day.'
Yvonne, 40, librarian, Leeds.

'Her references seemed so good, then a week into the job, I discovered her last 'boss' had been the girl she shared a squat with and the glowing reference and follow-up phone call were also from her.'
Anne, 38, beautician, Streatham.

'I came home and found the house in chaos and the children so worked up with excitement they had temperatures. When she said she loved playing with children, I didn't think she meant *all* day.'
Marianne, 35, pharmacist's assistant, Orpington.

'She had been with us a couple of weeks and we were at friends for dinner when she phoned to ask where we kept the fire extinguisher.'
Lynn, 36, secretary, Falkirk.

I expect you've heard worse. Certainly I have. The nannies and mother's helps and au pairs who regard the phone as their own but the bill exclusively yours, who borrow your clothes, drink your drink, seduce the window cleaner in your bed and just about the only thing you don't get around to rowing about is your children in her care whose names she frequently forgets. You've probably also heard the saying, 'She eats like an au pair'. It is not a joke.

There are, of course, carers who are paragons of propriety, who love your children to bits, make you feel like a homecoming hero the minute your key turns in the lock and never let their charges out of their sight for a second.

'Marlene stayed for four years. She was terrific. But then I made it difficult for her to go. I would cry pitifully and noisily if she even thought about it, increase her salary to a small fortune and, if that didn't seem to work, I cheerfully used blackmail. Anything, so long as she stayed.'
Maureen, 40, architect, Arbroath.

'She was superb, but I suspected she was getting fed up with the way the kids messed up the house. So over the weekend I really spring-cleaned. By Monday, the house was spotless, the children on their best behaviour, a smell of fresh coffee wafted through the open door. It worked, she stayed.'
Cathy, 30, media buyer, Barnes.

More words have been written on childcare than Penthouse has devoted to sex. And for a very good reason. You cannot, *absolutely cannot*, cut corners on this one.

Let me put this to you: A strange man comes to the door in response to an advertisement to buy your car. Do you, (a) let him take it for a trial spin on his own, or (b) insist your partner goes with him?

Or what about this: A colleague of your husband's – whom he hardly knows – asks to borrow his car for the weekend. Does your husband (a) hand over the keys because he doesn't want to offend him, or (b) refuse, saying he might when he knows him better?

The answers are so obvious and so obviously right. No, you wouldn't let a stranger take your car for a trial run and no, your husband wouldn't hand over the keys, until he knew his colleague better.

So why is it that every day hundreds of mothers – and fathers – hand over their children to a virtual stranger with far less qualms and with only a couple of references that they haven't even bothered to investigate properly?

Not so long ago, a small child was abducted when the baby minder had 'seemed so nice'. No references were taken up, no phone calls made, no-one checked with Social Services. Thankfully, the baby was found and returned to her distraught parents.

Unless you are one of the rare and fortunate people who discovers one of the equally rare companies that provides a creche for the under fives, you will be hunting for childcare on your own.

Finding the right person to care for the kids might *seem* easy, but believe me it isn't. Along with half my friends, I believed it would be a doddle – but as I worked my way through the applicants I joined my friends in being convinced that the world is full of deranged women with delusions of grandeur.

Like the woman who came in reply to my first-ever ad for a 'nanny'. 'And where,' she boomed, looking scathingly around the tiny living room of my small London house, 'are the nursery, kitchen and bathroom?'

Then there was the woman who plonked herself down, proceeded to take out her knitting and, without pausing for breath, told me she liked to have the place to herself, preferred no interference from me while she was on duty and went on to highlight several reasons why grandparents should be discouraged from just dropping in. I encouraged her to drop out of my life immediately.

Another lasted until midday the day after she started because I could no longer bear to hear her endlessly prattling on about how it was when she worked for Danny Kaye.

From all this you will have grasped that I didn't really know what I was looking for. And you're right. Finding the right help, someone who will be 'you' while you're out of the house, is about as easy as finding a penthouse on Park Lane at a council flat rent.

There are four main categories of carers to choose from, and although they might appear to be the same thing, they are quite different:

Live-in nannies are qualified women whose job it is to care for your child and nothing else. The most expensive of all categories, generally speaking they're great for babies and children up to school age. But they don't come cheap and they see their role as strictly to look after the children. So any ideas you might have of a little light housework

39

or a quick trip to Tesco is out, unless it's strictly for something to do with the children.

They mostly live in, which has its advantages, but they must be given their own 'reasonable' room, live as one of the family (unless it's in a very grand house in which case it's unlikely the chatelaine is too bothered about returning to work) and have generous time off – usually a minimum of one evening a week, one day each weekend and one complete weekend once a month.

Some only want to live in during the week, others want a firm set of hours to work within which means, unless you have pre-arranged it, they don't like still being on duty at eight at night, having started at 7am, while you drop in to the local wine bar on the way back from work.

If they go on holiday with you, in order for you to have a rest, that cannot be counted as their own holiday – and it really is mean to put a padlock on the fridge to keep the food bills down if they appear to have a bit of an appetite.

Find them through domestic and specialist agencies, and training schools. The phone book is by far the best source for numbers, or the magazine *The Lady*, which lists agencies that should be reliable. Warning: Even if the candidate comes with a personal recommendation from Mother Teresa herself, and the agency swear they've already done it, take up all their references again. And never employ someone who is enthusiastic about finger paints and creative play as in, 'Let's find a new word in *The Sunday Times*, shall we'. Oh *c'mon*, you wouldn't, would you?

Live-in mother's helps are just like nannies but are expected to help with light household chores as well as the children. Mostly they don't get paid as much as a nanny, which I agree sounds odd since they are doing more. But they usually have no formal training and, unless they have had children of their own, you really should think twice about leaving very tiny babies in their care, no matter how 'natural' they seem to be with them.

If you are going to be absent all day, it is not a good idea to have a mother's help who is still in her teens. Of course she'll agree to it, but half the time she really won't have a clue what to do if the baby is unwell or keeps on screaming. She should be hired only if you are going to be around a lot so that she can assist you with the running of house and family.

Non-residential nannies and mother's helps are much the same, except that they go home at night and don't (usually) work at weekends. You'll probably find you'll pay more in actual salary, but in the end it works out the same since you have to feed and board the ones who live in. Having said that, some mother's helps who live out can be a bit cheaper, particularly if they live locally and don't have to worry about fares and can be back home within ten minutes at the end of the day.

In my own case, because I worked from home for a long while, I didn't need a proper 'nanny' but a daytime mother's help, a nice, kindly, funny but firm lady who would love the kids to pieces and take me to her heart.

Actually I was looking for Mary Poppins. I expect you are too…

I will now save you a great deal of work. She doesn't exist. But if you're lucky you will find one of those wonderful, winning women who in their different ways all produce excellent results; and if you get the right one (as I did, not once but twice, and both Kathleen and Sharon are still regarded as very much part of our family) they will become the bedrock of your life.

Quite different from a nanny, these are the women who, you hope, will love the kids, be nice to their friends, do some light housework and the ironing and shopping. A car driver is really useful.

The trick to keeping them happy and therefore keeping them is to take into account *their* lives, what they like and don't like doing and, provided you are all agreed that the children come first, to compromise on other areas.

If she clearly gets on well with the kids, is prepared to do the housework but hates shopping, then do the shopping yourself. If she is cheerful, adores the kids, loves taking them shopping and on outings, but absolutely loathes ironing… Well, it's worth biting the bullet for peace of mind.

You must respect that they have their own lives to lead and, whatever you do, don't move the goalposts once they're established – unless you're prepared to pay a little more.

Au pairs. These part-time helpers are almost exclusively foreign, will stay for up to a year and are expected to spend some time studying. Usually the most exploited group, since they are paid little more than pocket money in return for board and lodging and some help in the house including baby-sitting. They are not meant to be left in sole charge of your children from morning until night but some employers unscrupulously regard them as poorly paid slave labour.

There are, however, some au pairs who consider they should be waited on hand and foot and who regard the smallest request as a gross imposition which they immediately report to their agency. Some have been known to ring national newspapers with tales of slave labour to rival scenes in *Gone With The Wind*.

Getting some basic ground rules sorted out *beforehand* is by far the most sensible approach. Au pairs can usually be found through agencies or by advertising in a reputable magazine like *The Lady*, which also lists au pair agencies.

There is another category here, and I'm not sure what you would call it, but it is strictly for older children – 11 to early teens. For a while we had two or three really smashing girls on a short term basis, who were travelling the world and stopping off to build up their resources and see something of the country. There were Raylene (Raz) from Australia, Cheryl from South Africa and Rhonda from New Zealand, and all had a responsible but easy-going kind of camaraderie with my children.

They aren't exactly cheap, but they are tremendous fun and for older children good value for the long summer breaks when they want to swim, play tennis, go on day trips with their friends, together with someone who is more like a big sister than a minder and can join in with their activities.

If you're in London, New Zealand House in the Haymarket has a board crammed full of names and addresses of girls looking for such employment. However, just because they are travelling doesn't mean you don't need references. *You do. You do. You do.*

Childminders are regulated for the care of children under eight in their own homes for more than two hours a day in return for payment, and are registerered with the Social Services. But they can also take older children within reason as long as this does not affect the care of the younger ones.

These women (rarely men) have met all the Social Services' very strict requirements about looking after children in their own homes. You take your kids to them and collect them at the end of the day. They charge anything from £50 to £80 per week, depending on the number of hours involved.

Perhaps the only drawback of a childminder is that it can be a real hassle getting buggies and perhaps even a carry-cot, together with small children, over to their house early in the morning – especially if you have a bus or train journey to negotiate. It can be a long day for your child, and at the end of it you have all that to look forward to again – getting back home.

On the other hand, the safety factors built into a registered childminder are of the most stringent kind. There are very strict and very reassuring guidelines on becoming registered, and not everyone is accepted on to the council's list as suitable to look after other people's children.

Social Services run a very thorough check on anyone who applies to be a childminder, plus a police and social services check is carried out on anyone in her family over the age of 16. The minder herself has to have a health check (which Social Services arrange) and the premises are inspected regularly to make sure they maintain the standard required on registration.

After that, some personal judgement must influence the decision, but it must still be a gentle, careful process. No-one should leave their child with someone they have met only once at the interview. The 'handover' should be done in stages, with the mother nearby to take over if the child is not settling easily: try half an hour the first time and then build it up over a few days.

You will find that most women who register as childminders make no objection whatsoever to the checks being run, and in fact welcome them. (Quite a sizeable number of qualified nannies are now also keen to have the same stringent checks done on them – such a properly registered list of nannies would go some way to eliminating the extra risk factor attached to employing someone to work in your own home.)

However, it is still possible to hear of lousy minders who do the absolute minimum required, so it is up to you to see several before you decide who is right for your child and to check out some basic facts for yourself.

Do you feel comfortable in her home? Does your child? If they keep a dog is it under proper control and do you mind? More important, does your child? Is there sufficient space for children to play?

Ask to see the loo and the kitchen. If your child is still at the age where he needs a rest in the afternoon, is there a suitable quiet place? Are all the other children being cared for at the baby stage while your child is seven or eight? Will your child feel comfortable with the rest of the family, especially if there are much older children around?

I've never been convinced that what people say and do always amounts to the same thing, so in the end you will have to fall back on your instincts for your final choice of minder. Unlike employing someone to work in your own home, you have to fit in with the childminder's routine and this can be hard if you and your child are creatures of habit.

In any event, make sure you take your child at least two or three times to meet the prospective minder in her home before making the big decision about leaving them with her.

The interview: choosing a carer

As a race, we shy away from asking personal questions, think it vulgar to talk about money and quite easily allow ourselves to be bossed into something we don't want because we can't bring ourselves to say no. Part of the reason why the majority of us get finding help so hopelessly wrong the first time round is that it is likely to be our first experience of interviewing and hiring someone. Still, mistakes are a simple way to gain experience.

But while you're reinventing yourself as a working woman, the person who is going to be there for your children, whether the highly-paid nanny, the competent, experienced mother's help or the childminder, is the one who'll have to fetch and carry, cuddle and comfort, toast the triumphs and commiserate with the calamities. Obviously, then, questions must be asked, and very personal questions at that.

With a nanny or mother's help, make all the enquiries you want to, just as the agency enquired of you at your interview. Don't shy away from asking about her personal circumstances because, where a child's safety is concerned, no question is too personal. Without the kind of interview skills used by trained Social Services' representatives in selecting childminders, you will have to rely very much on your own instincts. But if they have suddenly deserted you, try some of these: What are her views on food, travel, politics? Does she have a general childcare philosophy? What does she watch on TV and what would she do if your child fell off the fence and banged his head quite badly – or if he refused to eat? Somewhere along the line (without asking any direct questions) you will discover if she is married, divorced, single or has kids of her own. What about her views on race discrimination, and how much a child should be allowed to do unsupervised?

While she is talking to the children, ask yourself whether you like the tone of voice she uses with them, whether she seems to know how most children behave with strangers. Very important, too, does she recognise the characters they love best: Hulk Hogan or WWF Wrestling or Sonic Hedgehog?

It is important that you take up not just one, but two or even three references, particularly if the candidate is coming to you from another part of the country. If you feel embarrassed about asking someone who is obviously very nice – or seems it – you could always say, 'You seem so nice and suitable, I really can't imagine it will be necessary, but I know my husband/partner/mother will want to see some references'. Personally, I also feel it is imperative to make sure that a potential minder has a clean bill of health to avoid any medical problem being passed on to your children: ask them to supply a medical note from their doctor.

Every single candidate is nice at their interview and will promise the earth. Sometimes they deliver what they promise, more often they don't. So suggest a month's trial on either side. Make it clear right from the beginning what you are going to pay, whether that includes holidays and sick pay, or whether you will pay only for the days she actually works. Never get roped into paying by the hour unless on a very limited basis: it can be daylight robbery. Arrange a reasonable salary instead, possibly one that may be generous during term-time but will reflect the longer hours required during school holidays, half term and odd days away from school.

And give yourself some leeway on times. If you get home at six, ask if she can stay until 6.30 (or, if she's living in, stay on duty until then) to give you a breathing space to change and have a quick cup of tea before you take over.

Don't encourage live-out minders to take the children to their house and look after them there. Two problems arise if you agree to this: firstly, if her salary covers ironing and light housework she won't get this done, and you are likely to end up doing it yourself and, secondly, the children will soon get fed up because overall they are better off at home with their own toys, TV and friends around them.

Even if they don't live in, make it part of their job at least to begin to prepare supper before they go. If they are exclusively looking after your children (a nanny in fact), then you won't be able to enforce that one but, frankly, asking someone to peel a few potatoes or make a salad or wash some vegetables or have already phoned the home delivery pizza service is not, in my view, such an outrageous demand. While I'm all for understanding that she has her own life to live, if she has agreed to work until six o'clock and then starts pushing the time she leaves forward to five thirty, because her husband expects his tea on the table the minute he gets in or her boyfriend is waiting on the corner, then that is her problem.

You are not asking for charity, you are paying her. You couldn't do it in your job, could you? Do not get involved. Insist she stays until six. As to personality, a quiet withdrawn person is no good. Honestly. The kids and you both need someone who is jolly. You'll just have to put up with it if they are talkative. Far better, believe me, than someone unnervingly serene who smiles quietly all the time.

Most important of all: anyone you get must be prepared to *listen* to the children, to ask about their day at school, to give them a cuddle and, if they have to chastise them, to do it in the same way you would. They have got to have the right to tick them off, provided you have both agreed what form this is to take. Frankly, sending a small child to their room until you get home is babarous, smacking out of the question; but sanctions such as being deprived of a treat are perfectly reasonable.

Make sure your children are around for at least some of the interview and take their feelings into account. After all, how would you like it if you were left all day with someone who made you feel uncomfortable?

You, too, must stay tuned into your child. If you suspect they are feeling uneasy, or seem unusually withdrawn, and if they complain about whoever is minding them, don't let it go on for an instant.

Because, no matter how inconvenient, no job, no amount of money, no high-flying career is worth sacrificing a child's security on the altar of work.

It is reasonable and sensible to hire anyone you employ *at least* two weeks before you actually start work. You should never leave your child with someone they have only met once or twice before, and this applies equally to the childminder vetted by the Social Services.

In fact, it's far better all round that you all have a chance to get to know each other well before you start your new working life.

Young teenagers

There is of, course, a slightly more troublesome area to deal with and that is: who will look after young teenagers? A granny could come in useful here, but even grannies are no match for the charm of the persuasive teenager, so it is important to make sure you all understand the rules and stick by them: straight home from school, unless otherwise discussed (dawdling along, going to a friend's house, being lured into the amusement arcade, are the usual distractions – if there is an empty house ahead the temptation is even greater); homework must be done before *Neighbours* and *Home and Away*; and having hordes of friends piling into the house because they know granny is too soft to refuse is just not on. Nor, can you bet your life, will granny be, if she has to cope with that. Neither is whining behind each other's backs. Curiously enough, most children enjoy coming home to granny after school and it's an odd granny who doesn't welcome the chance to see her grandchildren on a regular basis.

So that things are fair, you should insist on contributing financially to the extra food she'll be forking out and reimbursing her for anything she pays for on your offspring's behalf. She might object to cash, in which case you should offer payment in another form: a visit to the hairdressers, her weekly shopping, a special treat. No-one, no matter how kind or close, should be expected to help out for nothing.

If there's no granny, aunt or friend available, it might be worth asking a neighbour to monitor the kids in from school and to raise the alarm if they don't see them by a reasonable time; or perhaps a friend's mother will be able to drop them home. A quick knock on the neighbour's door or some other pre-arranged signal might well be all you need, plus a check call to you at work to say they're safely in.

Another option is the older, responsible student who will 'child-sit' for a couple of hours after school and keep a friendly eye on them. You might have a turnover of helpers every few months – what I called the 'travellers' – but at that age it really isn't disruptive. Quite the reverse, it can be stimulating.

Most teenagers really can't stand the thought of having to go to someone else's house after school every day, so if they are over 13 and someone can see them safely in, or at least check that they have arrived home, you might be better off trusting them not to set the house alight. Ring from work to make sure they're there, and make another check an hour or so later.

Bunking off school when there is no-one to monitor them is common, so you should make sure that the school knows you are working and that any unexplained absences should be reported to you. And you *must* act on it. If you are suspicious (forged 'absent' letter are not unknown) then check at the next parents' evening or make a discreet call to the class teacher. (Don't make a big thing of it to the head – defusing situations at the point where everyone is still speaking to each other is more valuable than a major confrontation.)

It is my personal view that, unless you desperately need to go back to work, you should delay your return if your child is taking important exams. On the other hand, we are not talking here about eight-year-olds but children who, we hope, have had good sense drummed into them, are not going to get in with the most unsavoury gang in the neighbourhood and are not likely to turn your home into a den of drug trafficking, or worse. And some teenagers relish the idea of coming into an empty house where they can enjoy working their computer, watching TV or playing James or Megadeth even louder than usual. There are even those (perhaps more than you think) who just want the chance of studying in a quiet house with no-one to interrupt or nag them.

During winter months, when they'll be arriving home at dusk or after dark, it's a good idea to have a light on so that they can see it as they come in. That, and a welcoming light snack left in the fridge and they're unlikely to be too bothered whether you're there or not!

When you can't afford childcare
Of course, it's no help that government childcare support is abysmal in

this country, but they are pledged to create 50,000 more nursery places over the next few years, which is a move in the right direction. Some companies do provide a creche for the under-fives and some excellent organisations such as Kids Club Network (071 247 3009) have a very thorough updated nationwide directory on what schemes are available to get you through holidays, days off school and the after-school period.

But I do urge you (and this is backed by every concerned association) to think long and hard about letting very young children walk home alone after school, or to spend unsupervised days in the house when you are out working.

No matter how bright, how thoughtful, how sensible you think they are, in reality very few children are sophisticated enough to handle a situation they have never encountered before. Could they really cope with knowing you are not going to be there when they get in – and being trusted not to open the door to anyone? Do they really know the quiet, dodgy roads to avoid, how to use a crossing, the importance of not wandering off to a friend's house without telling you?

Only you know what your child is capable of. But why not ask their class teacher for their view of your child's maturity and ability to handle a crisis before you decide? Again, you could try finding out whether another mother who walks past your house/gets the same bus would be willing to drop your child off, making sure they are safely in. Best of all, ask yourself whether it really is out of the question to find someone to keep an eye on them until you get home and, if so, should you really, therefore, be working?

Tracking down the minder

Given that you are in the market for a childminder, finding the right person depends on what you want. You don't necessarily pay your money and take your choice, so don't be mislead into thinking that the more expensive and demanding the prospective nanny or mother's help, the better they will be. On the other hand, it is not wise to employ someone simply because they are cheaper.

Advertisements: If you want day-time help only, try putting an ad in the local paper rather than a national or county paper. That way you are more likely to get a local person who can drive and is familiar with the area, the schools, the shops, and won't take hours to get to you each day. Work out what you can afford, ring round a few ads already in the paper and find out what they are paying. That way you will get a rough idea of the going rate.

What do you say in the ad? The truth for a start. Don't describe your home as luxurious if it is simply comfortable. Saying you keep other help doesn't count if the other help is your mother who comes once a month to do a good clean-through: you'll simply end up wasting your time interviewing someone who will take one look at your idea of luxury and extra help and vanish into the blue.

Don't give too many details. Just explain what you are looking for, the hours, whether live-in or live-out, car driver essential or not, non-smoker, the ages of your children and a phone number – but for very obvious reasons *never* give their names as well as a phone number. On the other hand, beware of 'cuteness':

'Our three gorgeous children are just longing to meet you? Would you like to care for an enchanting trio of boisterous children while I pop out to work?' or

'A former Miss Pears contestant and still as scrumptious, is looking for a loving, caring, mummy substitute' or – and here I must ask you to pass the motion disturbance bag:

'I am leaving it to a charming little rogue of eight and a future heart-breaker of 11, to decide who shall mind them while I work. Please call me to make an appointment to meet them.'

You might think ads like these would rule out applicants who can't manage the hours, smoke like chimneys, have had their licence taken away and can't stand cute kids. Well it won't, it will only discourage a few.

But the ones who do apply will already have decided you're so unreal it's worth pushing the deal their way. Some will try to alter the hours. (One or two might try to re-negotiate your children's view on life.) Remember you are hiring someone to solve your problems, not theirs. So stick to real life.

<u>Agencies</u>: If you get the right agency with a solid reputation then they will bend over backwards to meet your needs and not rest until they do. However, as in all these things, there are the bad who trade on the name of the good, so ring and ask them their fees before you even start to talk about hiring someone. Remember, before sending you a candidate for interview they will ask you to register; the fee can vary from £10-£50, and you don't get it back.

Don't be intimidated by agencies. They have to make a living – and a crisp, confident voice (rather than an apologetic one) that tells them they are asking way above what you expect to pay, may well make them prepared to be a bit more realistic and understand your needs more closely.

Again, be careful about dealing with agencies until you have checked *them* out. I know, I know, I know, they mostly *do* vet their staff, but they can be very expensive and one or two are a complete rip-off. First of all, they all charge commission – and are they tough about it! – and they can stuff fanciful ideas into the heads of their workers regarding salary and conditions, irrespective of their qualifications. In the early days I found myself interviewing candidates whose experience of children appeared to be derived solely from having once been a child themselves but who were demanding the salary of a fully qualified Norland Nanny.

You'll probably find that these days a lot of mother's helps – and nannies too – prefer to work on a daily basis and live out. For most of us that is the ideal solution, especially if you can come to an arrangement where they will baby-sit for a bit of extra loot when you need them. Continuity of help is terribly important for children, especially the under-tens who thrive on the security it represents.

For a live-out mother's help, provided you are prepared to scrutinise their references with the ferocity of a VAT inspector, you will probably find someone locally, without getting involved in agency fees and advertisements: ask everyone from the local vicar to neighbourhood nursery schools. Ideally, you want someone with a grown-up family, who isn't tied to school hours and who wants to work locally.

Local health centres or the district health visitor plus local women's groups are also good sources. It's a matter of trial and error, because you will find lots of pleasant ladies and young women who want the job but can't do the right hours or don't want to do the housework –

but there just may be someone who wants to do both.

Beware young mums with young children of their own. Be careful here. This might sound the perfect solution, particularly if your's love babies and toddlers. But the reality is that if one of their's goes down with a cold/chickenpox/something they ate, or needs ferrying around, your needs and your child's, will come second. And if their child is only a few months old, they may well not be getting enough sleep and feel worn out before they even get to your boisterous brood.

Granny figures? Should be approached with caution unless it's your own granny, and even then think twice. Okay if you're only going to be working part time, but if you're away all day, older people can forget just how demanding young children are mentally and physically, how exhausting the whole business of caring for them can be.

Friends on the cheap? Hmm. Avoid them if you can. If your children get on their nerves, or they get on your children's nerves, you might end up without a beautiful friendship.

Beyond choosing someone you hope will be the right person, you're on your own as far as <u>financial arrangements</u> go, and that must include paying tax and national insurance for anyone you are employing who is earning more than the government's minimum earnings limit. Some people simply ignore those requirements, particularly if the person they employ just wants some extra cash to supplement the family income, but be warned: the full weight of the tax office will come crushing down on both of you if you are discovered dodging tax. Sorting out sick pay is a very complex subject – and one that frankly needs a personal chat with the DSS about what you are and are not supposed to do. I suggest calling them (0800 393539) and getting it from the horse's mouth.

Whoever you decide to hire, if they can only work until 5.30 and you won't get home until six, forget them. Don't even think about trying to re-negotiate your hours at work to accommodate their needs, or worse, try a desperate dash home every night only to be greeted by Dottie/Mabel/Mona standing in the doorway, pointedly looking at her watch and ready to negotiate more money for the 'extra'. Likewise, if you take your child to a childminder don't exploit her by constantly turning up late to collect your child. If it's unavoidable (train delayed, bus held up) no-one will mind, but if you know you are going to be late, try to phone or let her know in advance.

Keep in mind that daily nannies/mother's helps who answer local ads are not going to be ambitious career women. Generally, they are looking for extra money, are fond of children and want something that isn't too demanding or unfamiliar. Most are women who have brought up their own families, can cook and clean, and just want to do the same for someone else, but with the novelty of money and gratitude thrown in.

Don't expect them to stay forever; after all, everyone's circumstances change, you move house, change jobs, win the pools. All kinds of things alter our lives for us.

When it happens – and it will – don't feel resentful. If she's served you well and stayed for a long time, she deserves thanks not irritation, unless of course she's leaving taking your husband with her. That, of course, is quite another matter…

YOU CAN WORK IT OUT

Chapter Five

D on't let anyone undermine your ambition. Avoid discussing your plans with those who are lazy or apathetic, who tell you you're wasting your time, there aren't any jobs, you're too old/too tall or anything else this bunch of under-achievers can dream up to zap your insecurity. There's nothing wrong with feeling thirty, especially if you're pushing forty.

These days it is necessary to push twice as hard for half the jobs, and only those who really feel motivated are going to get there. Motivation is a strong word, but it's what we all need most of the time just to get out of bed in the morning. Try this:

Question: Your best friend offers your name as organiser of the next fund raising dinner at school/church/the tennis club. Your reaction is:
a) You feel quietly pleased, but modestly suggest they might need someone with more experience
b) You feel panic stricken and think it only fair to come clean and tell them about that business when the emergency services had to come and put out the blaze caused by the barbecue you were organising at the summer fete
c) You love the idea but say, obviously you'll have to consult your husband's schedule, and make sure it doesn't clash with your youngest's karate class
d) You agree, saying you know how hard it is to get someone to take on these tasks, and ask how many others they have asked before you
e) You decide it was your intimidatingly high profile locally that had made them ask you first.

Assessment: When you decide to go back to work the ground rule is: never sell yourself short. So while answer (**e**) is grade A self confidence, it is the one most likely to get you back to work on pretty well your own terms.

If you were excruciatingly honest and answered (**b**) you can be quietly pleased that honesty is a wonderful policy, but if you want to get a job, why didn't you mention how you were the first to raise the alarm and organise the emergency services when they arrived?

55

On the other hand, (**a**) isn't such a bad answer. Just drop the idea that someone else might do whatever job you're after better than you. Maybe they could, but draw attention to everyone else's abilities, if you really must, *after* you've clinched the deal.

If you answered (**c**) you might not be able to make the psychological leap out of the house. You're certainly thoughtful but you still don't feel equal.

And (**d**) doesn't make you sound very confident. What on earth makes you think you were so far down the list of candidates? Start assuming you were first.

We all need to feel motivated to do something with our lives. But that doesn't mean we have to be like those searingly boring women who talk endlessly about achieving targets and setting goals for themselves and only end up sounding like overworked slot machines in an amusement arcade.

The motivation that is most likely to get you back to work in a job that means something centres on how you look and how you feel. Only then will you have the confidence to walk purposefully into a job looking like you know what you're doing.

This does not mean having an unshakeable belief that your whole life will start to make sense if you can just find the right dress, but it just might if you rethink the tracksuit and sling out all those clothes you'll never wear again (I swear to you, those platforms will never make a re-entry; the new versions are *nothing* like the ones you bought ten years ago). It might if you aim to lose eight pounds in a month, devise your gameplan to start when the children go back to school and let your ex's new wife regret she ever lured him away when you lay it on him that he's got to have the kids eight weekends in a row while you retrain.

In a busy, already overburdened life it is difficult to find time to do everything, but convince yourself that in three weeks you will have started the diet, promised never again to exceed the feed limit (even if it is only wishful thinking), had your hair cut, organised a childminder, and I bet you by the end of the month you will be powering your way through the sits vac and storming the employment agencies. It's getting the foothills out of the way that makes the mountain seem easier to scale. I think.

Keep your ambitions on a realistic level. Don't apply for a job that asks for skills or qualifications way beyond those you possess, but don't aim so low that you end up not getting the job because you are over qualified.

What disappoints most women returners is finding that the field they once excelled in now has the wrong hours or no suitable entry level, that the job they left may not be the one they are going back to or might mean far too much retraining. But that doesn't mean to say you have nothing to offer. It just means calling upon the skills you have accrued since you gave up work and rethinking the job you trained to do; for instance, is there another element to it that would suit you now and which would mean not having to abandon the field completely?

Quite often the biggest stumbling block to finding out what you can do is that you yourself have changed: your perspective is different; what once seemed important no longer matters; what you once enjoyed doing now bores you rigid.

The girl who loved being on reception, who enjoyed meeting new people and the whole social side of office life, and who was content to leave all the detailed paperwork to others, might now be the woman who finds researching the responses to a new product completely fascinating.

If you spent your pre-children years buried in cataloguing the 'Encyclopedia of Atomic Energy', fully absorbed in developments at Sizewell and Sellafield, it might come as a shock to discover that these days you get a real buzz from being a leading light at the local party political office.

And what about your communication skills? Where once you found it impossible even to phone the bank manager to discuss your overdraft, these days you have no trouble asserting yourself, from questioning the treatment your GP is giving you to telling your husband why you're three hours late coming back from your best friend's hen night. By the time you've sorted out the answers to the following few questions, you might find that, without knowing it, you have succeeded in reinventing yourself.

What kind of woman have you become and what type of work are you cut out for:

1. You're off on a week's holiday to a deserted beach: what will you take to read?
a) The latest best-selling fiction and a stack of Sunday supplements
b) A favourite book of poems, the latest New York novel and a bit of science fiction
c) Biographies and a first aid manual
d) 'The Complete Dickens' or 'The Works of William Shakespeare'
e) An armful of the latest pulp best-selling paperbacks.

2. You have the decorators in. The most trying aspect of the upheaval is:
a) Persuading them that you really do want a raspberry border in a grey bathroom when they want to paint everything white
b) Deciding how far down the walls the grapevine stencilling can come
c) Keeping the workmen to a deadline
d) Living with the invasion of privacy and turmoil of upside-down rooms
e) Resisting the urge to make them another cup of tea and have a chat.

3. You meet a friend for lunch at the office where you used to work and a lot has changed; it's wall to wall computers now. Is your first reaction:
a) This must make life a lot easier – no more filing cabinets
b) I wonder how much time they spend playing Super Mario
c) It's like a space station: I'd need a refresher course before I could even think of returning
d) I'd like all this at home so I'd never have to come out to an office
e) I'm not sure I could figure out how to turn a computer on – there must be somebody around to help.

4. Christmas, a friend's wedding, a 25th anniversary and the school pageant are all happening in one week this year. Do you immediately:
a) Start making lists of things to do in order of priority, write everything in a main diary but keep separate event planners, delegate chores early and post a chart on the kitchen wall so you can see at a glance what you've done and what's still needed

b) Plan all the decorations, buy and wrap the presents, make place settings and arrange the centrepiece before you even think of how to be in two places at once

c) Work out the budgets, refuse to take on the wedding catering, but agree to sort out baby-sitting details and arrange accommodation for out-of-town guests

d) Feel faint at the prospect of swarms of people and plan to go abroad for Christmas week

e) Plan to introduce the guests to each other at each separate event and wrap up the week with a big party.

5. You get a series of obscene phone calls at home. Do you:
a) Hang up immediately – what is there to say?
b) Keep a whistle by the phone and let loose a piercing blast at the next one
c) Get an ex-directory listing
d) Get angry and call the police; you feel your privacy's been invaded
e) Feel puzzled that anyone wastes their time and energy doing this.

6. You round the corner and find a crowd of people milling around the scene of a car accident. Do you:
a) Dial 999 immediately on your portable phone, quickly find out, from the victim if possible, what's happened and explain it all to the paramedic when he arrives
b) Find the incident both upsetting and fascinating, watching how different people react to the drama
c) Size up the injuries and get the first aid kit from your car boot; mop up a bit of blood and cover the victim with a warm blanket
d) Walk past the crowd and the accident. You're not a trained medical person and would rather not get involved
e) Hold the victim's hand until the ambulance arrives and offer to go with them to the hospital since they seem to be on their own.

7. If you are feeling down and need something to shake off depression, would you:
a) Write out your feelings in your diary or journal – and some positive resolutions too

59

b) Splurge on a fantastic new season's outfit or a ridiculously expensive pair of shoes
c) Turn out a few cupboards, dig the garden, wallpaper a room
d) Take a solitary hike through the woods
e) Round up as many friends as possible and invite them over for wine and gossip.

8. You've thrown a huge party on New Year's Eve, always a time of high expectations. When it's finally over, what do you remember as the best bit?
a) The way you kept guests circulating, introductions flowing, weeded out wallflowers, brought like-minded people together
b) The marvellous decorations and the good food
c) The way you costed it down to the last penny and still had a bottle of Champagne left over, and arranged transport so that everyone got home safely
d) Being grateful that you scrapped the party when the list started to grow and settled for a couple of old friends and a bottle of rosé instead
e) The way you managed to dance with everyone and how they all said it was the best party they'd been to in years.

9. You're invited to an important party and have to buy a new dress. Do you:
a) Go all out on an outrageous but wonderful outfit, including the hat, because you're never shy of taking centre stage
b) Design and make your own dress because nothing you see in the shops expresses how you want to feel
c) Add up your pennies and sigh, and decide you'll have to settle for the second favourite outfit
d) Buy the first suitable thing that fits
e) Invite all your girlfriends to a 'Frockswop'. In exchange for wine and great gossip, you get to borrow one of the frocks.

How did you score?
<u>Mostly a's</u>: You're a communicator, good at expressing ideas, encouraging people and making them see things clearly. You're articulate and organized and like explaining things. You're a natural

teacher and would make a good social worker, saleswoman or office supervisor.

Mostly b's: You're the creative type with endless ideas, not always the most practical, not afraid of anything new and innovative, and very up-to-date in your thinking. You could be an artist, caterer, floral arranger, a fashion industry natural.

Mostly c's: You're the technical, cool-headed type who is realistic and practical and not afraid of a little hard work. You make your mark with anything involving computers, office management, finance, quality control.

Mostly d's: You're a loner, a bit shy, easily distracted by office gossip and unhappy with office politics. You'd love working from home (possibly with computer link-up) and would make a good librarian or researcher. You prefer to deal with products and items rather than people.

Mostly e's: You're the team player, outgoing, friendly, eager to fit in and work hard; not jealous of other people's ideas and loyal to your employer. You'd make an excellent office worker anywhere in the hierarchy from typing pool to senior management. You would also be a good nurse, receptionist, saleswoman.

Now you know what you can do – or should be doing – there are a whole host of organisations waiting to help. Some better than others. Some, frankly, quite useless.

'I went to the local job centre and they said I wasn't qualified for anything they had. I asked about retraining and they looked as though I had just asked for a single to Mars.'
Sylvia, 38, Sandhurst, Berks.

'I asked at the employment agency in the high street if they had anything that involved design. She said what about a receptionist at an engineering company? I said I preferred design. She said the engineering company didn't deal in design.'
Harriet, 35, Enfield.

But why didn't they say, but they knew someone who could retrain them, find a job in design or even set them up in a freelance capacity? Shortage of resources is what keeps most enthusiastic and enlightened

retraining groups from beating the drum about the courses they have –
those designed to help women with everything from regaining their
confidence to getting the job they want. The best of these are listed at
the back of the book.

So, from when you thought you couldn't do anything at all, a few
weeks later might prove you could run the world. Okay, maybe the
local job centre. But the very least you can do for other women is to
make sure your local library/school/church/job agency and, for what
it's worth, your local job centre, are stocked with leaflets from all
those retraining groups.

Remember you are not making up for lost time, this isn't a race. You
are starting a new job.

HOW TO GET THE BOSS YOU WANT
Chapter Six

'**E**veryone said just be yourself. So I was. I told him about Caroline getting a place at the grammar school, and what hell it was on the Northern Line, and how handy that supermarket on the corner would be for lunch time shopping. He didn't say anything except that he'd be in touch. I haven't heard a word.'
Michelle, 42, Warrington.

'He asked me how far I would go to get this job and I said no further than Marble Arch. He didn't laugh.'
Helen, 39, Chester.

'He said the department's work was confidential, could I handle that? I said, don't worry about a thing. I forget everything I'm told.'
Jackie, 40, Arbroath.

Never sell yourself short. Self-confidence is in short supply for most of us. But you've got to summon it up from somewhere. The feeling that this is the one time you are going to get caught out is quite common. Show me the man, or woman, who boasts they have never felt a moment's self doubt in their entire working life, and I will show you someone whose last grip on reality is either tenuous or has completely snapped.

Drop the idea that someone else might do whatever job you're after better than you. Maybe they could, but draw attention to everyone else's abilities *after* you've clinched the deal. *You* are the one to decide what you can offer, not some patronising interviewer or personnel officer (human resources they are sometimes called). Weigh up the options open to you, based on what you did before you had the children; and look at the skills you've accrued since.

It's no secret that all that's involved in raising a family and keeping everything running smoothly in the home could, on paper, sound exactly like the qualities needed for a company chairman who has to keep the workforce happy, encourage his chief executives to get along with each other and organise the firm's outing – all while trying to stop profit from turning into loss.

Most people find working a doddle. But I doubt there's anyone in the land who has ever approached the interview with anything like the confidence they have about actually doing the job. Before you've even got to the interview – in itself some feat these days – they will have your CV in their hands and, along with everything else, you've got to live up to it.

It helps, of course, to have written your CV along the lines of how it is, not how you would like it to be, although there's nothing wrong with massaging the truth a little or stretching a few salient points here and there. After all, everyone else does it, so don't go a goal behind before the game has even started.

They play such an important part of the selection process that there are even courses in how to prepare your CV, how to pump up a flat one and how to sell yourself without actually telling bare-faced lies.

You can say things in a CV which you might not get the opportunity to discuss at the interview, and which help create the right kind of impression before you even walk through the door: things like interests you may have or activities you enjoy.

'I enjoy the cinema, particularly films with a strong social issue' suggests you are thoughtful and caring. So what if Harrison Ford happened to star in the last three you've seen. Say, 'I enjoy reading, usually travel books', and there you are, a woman with broad horizons who is receptive to new ideas.

On the other hand, insights such as 'I enjoy walking and recently completed 20 miles raising money for charity' are not the most vital qualifications for an assistant in a market research company. But it certainly says that you are energetic and caring.

And although I agree that 'I do a lot of walking and recently completed 20 laps of Sainsbury's pushing a loaded trolley and was still able to smile when the youngest hurled the eggs to the floor as I reached the checkout' makes you sound a good humoured soul, it is not quite the right tone. It's unfair, I know, but it somehow makes you sound a bit neurotic.

So, too, does applying for a job on green, pink or mauve paper. Don't ask me why, it just does. Pretty cards or letter headings entitled 'Gossip from Grace' might be a real hoot to your friends, but they'll do little to make an impact on the head of sales at MegaMillion Mobiles.

Trying to decipher weird-coloured ink on silver paper will leave the recipient cross eyed, irritated and bewildered – and don't send a video of yourself, reams of 'samples of your work' (especially if the work was done some time ago) and a dossier detailing your life history. No-one nowadays is that interested or has the time to read a document starting, 'During my childhood in Cornwall…' and finishing eight pages later with, 'My youngest is now five and I know I will be a splendid addition to your team'.

Most employers used to receiving shoals of CVs are quick to recognise the ones that are playing around with unexplained gaps and feel uncomfortable before they've even got to finding out why you think you can do the job.

There is nothing wrong with having a career break. It's not a crime, and it can actually do a lot for your image. Far from believing that employers are nervous about taking on women with children, there are a fair few who would choose you over someone younger – who may land them with a seven-month gap for maternity leave. Someone who has completed their family is often seen as less of a risk. (I never said it was fair. Just fact.)

Avoid sounding vague or trying to disguise the fact that all your achievements are a few years out of date. Simply describe what you used to do, list your qualifications and explain why you think you are ready to take on reorganising the business plan at Sloth Brothers. Don't shrink from playing up your time at home – as long as you adopt a different standpoint to that of one high-powered new mother wishing to return to work. In her letter to a captain of industry she wrote: 'I love my child but I'm suffocating'. You could hear guilt and sobs pouring from it. No-one wants a guilt trip on their hands. No-one wants a woman who is returning to work because she's going mad at home. It might well be the truth, so unload on your best friend, your mother, write to Marje Proops – but on no account tell your prospective employer, even if she's female.

What she should have said was: 'After a break to have a child I am now preparing to resume my career. My skills for the job you advertise have been supplemented by the knowledge I accrued campaigning locally for improved nursery education' – or whatever she had been busy doing.

List down all the things you've done at home – running the PTA, voluntary work, belonging to the Housewives Register. Did you start to write a novel, campaign for anything, help at election time, join the Residents' Association? Anyone who has found time to participate locally is clearly a) energetic and organised, and b) familiar with planning and detailed work.

Of course, the experts on these things are the ones who are on the receiving end of CVs and job hunters every day of their lives in one way or another.

Charles Paterson, owner of Charles Paterson Search and Select, advises on executive appointments to some of the country's top industrial companies, including media conglomerates, advertising groups and those involved in new technology. He has a small, tight list of points he likes to see that will guarantee a CV wings its way to the right quarter – and nearer to an interview.

'Be truthful,' he advises. 'An experienced head-hunter will instantly recognise if someone is altering the facts. And don't try to cover up unexplained gaps. If you've been out of the job market for a while bringing up children, say so. There's no crime in that and, if the rest of the CV stands up, your chances of being put on a shortlist are just as good as the next person's.

'Personally I don't like to see a CV which charts a career promotion, say every two years, in a number of different companies. If you have to go elsewhere to be promoted, I ask myself why each of the companies you worked for did not recognise your abilities. It throws a question mark over your claims. Makes me reluctant to push such a candidate forward.

'Women returning to the job market? Same applies. Personally I would assume, if they have children, that they have worked out their domestic arrangements and I wouldn't even ask what they were.

'On the other hand, I wouldn't ignore the subject altogether. I always think it's a good idea to stick it on the CV, under personal details, "married, two children", which gets it out of the way.'

Jane Reed, Director of Corporate Affairs at News International, looks for a hint of the writer's personality in the style of the CV. Take note of what she says: Jane herself has risen through the ranks of editing magazines such as *Woman* and *Woman's Own* and ever upwards to the higher echelons of newspaper publishing where today, through sheer talent and hard work, not to mention a strong dose of realism, she has reached her current position within Rupert Murdoch's publishing arm in this country.

'I am frankly not all that impressed by a desk top publishing mini-magazine with photographs of the applicant plastered all over it – such as I received on my last recruitment campaign,' she says. 'But, oddly enough, a small, suitably serious picture of the applicant could be useful for a returner – just in case a sexist is drawing up a shortlist and feels that he would be unable to cast his eyes on any woman over 40!

'A badly presented letter and CV is off-putting. It shows a lack of self-esteem. If there are no recent professional milestones, then experience gained from life can tell you a lot about a person. Put down everything of relevance but not the stuff about the amateur dramatics with the WI – unless you directed them in a production of your own translation of Euripides.

'I also think it's important to assume in the tone of your letter that what you have been doing at home has been work and not some kind of leisure activity. Most women "at home" know a great deal more about the education system, the health service, public attitudes to retailing, street culture, youth employment, popular television, public transport and the voluntary service than any manager in a non-related business.

'I don't like bullshit – although a bit of enhancement shows enterprise. Me? Never had to write a CV until recent years when a head-hunter asked for one. It wasn't until then, when I was forced to write it down, that I realised so much was not just a list of jobs, but jobs and achievements within those jobs.'

Christine Walker is arguably the most influential woman in advertising today. As chief executive of Zenith Media, she is also a working mother who averages a twelve-hour working day. 'I never skimp on my nanny/au pair,' she says. 'They're too vital to mess around with.

'With regard to CVs, in my view the one influencing factor is the accompanying letter. I am always amazed at how little effort is put into the letter and how much time is spent including irrelevant details in the CV.

'Let me give you an example,' says Christine. 'We recently advertised in *The Daily Telegraph* for a research assistant. More than 400 people applied and the vast majority were rapidly rejected either because their letter was illegible, full of grammatical and spelling errors or, unforgivably, they got our company name wrong!

'Too many people also wrote pathetically off-target statements like, "I would like a job in advertising", when any research would reveal we are definitively a media specialist company. A real error is to attempt to grab attention by shocking. Being over the top is just as bad as being bland.

'I would wait and see if the subject of children comes up at interview. You may view this as irresponsible advice from the chief executive of a highly disciplined media company. However, the chances of being interviewed by someone who also happens to be a mother are extremely small. As a mother myself, I view it as irrelevant, but if it is mentioned, don't lie.

'Me? Actually I last wrote a CV in 1976 and can't remember!'

Watch your handwriting. Seriously. A number of top companies are now employing handwriting specialists to analyse just what those sloping letters reveal and whether your failure to complete your O's indicates whether or not you are team leader material.

Investment bankers SG Warburg and Co are one such company. Richard Hardie, a Director who has operational responsibility for 600 staff, finds it an invaluable insight into a candidate's suitability for the job. 'Everyone is told at interview that this is what will happen, but we don't reveal the result,' he explains. 'It may not be decisive but it is a really useful guide to traits not always obvious in an interview.'

It would, from that, be safe to assume that the best advice is not to have sleepless nights wondering how it is going to be interpreted, but to make sure your application is legible and spelled correctly.

Warburgs understand the value of women returning to work – particularly those with children – and are aware of how finely tuned their sense of commitment and responsibility tends to be.

'I never ask about their domestic arrangements,' says Richard. 'I just assume that, if someone has applied for a job, they must have that side of things worked out. In fact, married women with children are usually very organised – they have to be. So it would be very surprising to me if a new employee hadn't found that a very important aspect of returning to work.

'Curiously enough, we are attracting more married women to apply for some jobs than men. Computers and database management appeal to them, which is why I would recommend that any woman out of the job market for some time should familiarise herself with new techniques – former secretaries and clerical workers should update on new technology.'

And finally, to Jennifer D'Abo, the woman who took on the big players, hiked the stationers Rymans off them, sold out at a profit and now chairs one of the most exclusive floristry companies in the world, Moyses Stevens.

'As I have been a working mother, I can well understand why many mothers feel it is necessary to return to work,' she says. 'I think it's very important that as far as possible women are not stuck in a domestic environment 24 hours a day.

'I'm always impressed by women who return to full or part-time work even though they still have children at home but, having said that, I would be most concerned if they could not make assurances that their children would be well cared for while they were at work. It's not fair on either mother or child, if she's in a constant state of worry about what's happening at home while she's out working.'

Jennifer's much-admired career began when she sent out details of her career and ambitions in the form of a silver cut-out of the letters CV. She hoped this would impress the right people, and it worked: 'The bank who were interviewing me were so amused that they gave me the money to embark on my first business venture'.

That CV gimmick would, however, have made no dent at all if the business plan it contained was not perfectly sound and attractive. Jennifer knows that too.

'These days I prefer to see a CV laid out in neat paragraphs on plain paper with just the facts and a little bit about each job or work experience underneath. I don't feel photographs are at all necessary – the only person I have ever employed who sent me a photograph turned out to be a mistake. I am now very wary.

'I also feel that work experience is of far greater value than a string of degrees in subjects that do not relate to the job involved. Having a degree does not guarantee common sense!'

So there you are. What else? Plenty.

If the ad says, 'Please send recent picture', then of course you must. You must also resist the temptation to send one taken five years ago – or of someone else.

Simply the packaging of the CV can betray all kinds of things about you, or even worse, it can be misinterpreted. What was intended to be a witty, sophisticated letter can sound like the ramblings of a deranged housewife when read cold three days later, at nine in the morning, at NewDeals Incorporated.

Most companies like a handwritten covering letter on plain white paper (preferably A4). And you wouldn't believe how touchy people are about the spelling of their name. Geoffrey with a J, or Cathy with a K can tip the balance between you and someone else who bothered to get it right. So ring the company before you post off your CV. Double check the spelling and that you are sending it to the right person.

You may by now be wondering if there is a correct way to write a CV. Well, no there isn't. It's just common sense: your name, address, status, qualifications, skills, interests and references. Start, at the top of your career details, by saying what you were doing immediately prior to having your family, and then work backwards to your four 'O' levels from Wickhopton Grammar.

It's also a good idea to say from which date you would be available to start work should you be asked to join the company. I've known jobs to be swung to one candidate with nothing to choose between her and three others, because she was able to start promptly.

And now, what about the children? In theory, no-one is supposed to ask what plans you have about their daytime care while you devote yourself to Bought Ledger at NewDeals. But, in practice, most prospective employers feel reassured, as the above experts have testified, if they think you have all this organised.

Given the lousy state of childcare in this country, which we discussed earlier, and the lack of nursery school places, and also that many of Europe's big companies automatically have creches available to their parent workforce, in theory you should be able to say to them, 'And what do you propose to do about my children?'

However, while you could be forgiven for saying bluntly: 'I have two children and my friend, Sadie, is having them on Tuesday and Thursday, my mother-in-law will cover on Wednesday, and God alone knows what I'm going to do about Fridays', it is really better not to. Just state simply, 'I have two children and live-in daytime domestic help'. That covers everyone from Auntie Hilda to Caroline Strewth-Jones from Norland training school, and spares the employer from tying him or herself in knots, trying to elicit the information while not appearing prejudiced or intrusive.

And so here you are, it's the great day and you are on the shortlist, the only list, or the first candidate in. Who cares, you're in with a chance. The ad sounded wonderful or the agency said it was exactly you.

You've got the company's north east figures at your fingertips and the outfit you planned to wear is a knock-out number guaranteed to get results.

But as any working mother will tell you, the vision you have of turning up, on time, confident and cool is quite likely to be exactly that. A mirage.

The morning of the interview is bound to be the one when the four-year-old has thrown up twice the previous night, British rail has the wrong kind of leaves on the line and the school rings and says it's closing for the day because the pipes are frozen.

All of this must somehow be overcome. You should now put plan B into action. Plan B? *You don't know about Plan B?*

Plan B is what every working mother lives with. Some have the luxury of Plan C, and one woman I know even has Plan D. However, if I ever got to the stage of Plan C, I would query whether it was all worth it or just abandon the gameplan until the framework had been readjusted.

On the day of the interview you cannot afford this luxury. Plan B is the back-up team who move in when everything goes wrong. Auntie Hilda has gone down with flu? No problem (except for Auntie Hilda). Sadie said she would step in.

Whatever happens, you must be punctual, prepared for any eventuality and positive when you get there. Dress the part. Obviously, it would be unwise to take fashion trends too seriously and look as though you have dressed in front of an aeroplane propeller, but although no one wearing a bustier and hip-hugging mini-skirt is going to get the job as PA to director of research in a chemical company, as the receptionist at Glad All Over records it might be ideal. A padded shoulder power jacket, a pencil slim skirt and four inch stiletto heels is sure to send them racing for a pen to sign you up at Muggins Mirth Muggins Advertising Agency, but will reduce them to giggling wrecks at the local infants school.

Rule of thumb – unless you are absolutely certain a particular style of dress will go down well, stick to something simple, uncluttered and that won't get in the way: a clean-line, well-cut jacket, straight skirt, low heel pumps and a good haircut, cross all kinds of boundaries. Don't lug an important-looking briefcase with you unless it really has got necessary work or documents. Never, oh please, never, carry plastic shopping bags. The very thought practically overpowers me. Crossing and uncrossing your legs, smiling flirtatiously, licking your lipstick with your tongue, may well get you the job. But only for a while. It may not even be the job you thought you were after. But that's up to you.

If the interviewer is a woman... are you *mad?*

What advice would the experts give?

'I don't like bullshit,' says Charles Paterson. 'It doesn't impress me and I've heard it a hundred times before. There is an arrogance about it that suggests they think you are easily hoodwinked.'

Richard Hardie agrees: 'We don't like anyone who is too pleased with themselves but we do look for someone who can carry their point of view right through a meeting'.

Obvious exaggeration cuts no ice with Jennifer D'Abo, who says, 'I would be wary of anybody who claimed to have single-handedly set up and run a department – this would be the result of team work, not a solo performance.

'I would hope that at the interview any woman returning to work would leave me in no doubt that she wanted to be involved with my company and enjoy the work. In fact this is extremely important for the woman involved and for her workmates.

'I would be less likely to employ somebody who is totally uninterested in becoming involved and only wants the money. It's easy to spot if they know very little about the company and they show no interest in what we actually do.'

And what would stop Jane Reed giving someone a job? 'An air of desperation. Lack of awareness of what's going on in the world of work and in the particular sphere she's about to enter. It's quite insulting to find that the person you are talking to has no idea what the company does. Also nervousness about coping with her home circumstances. If she's decided to work I would expect her to have figured these out before she puts herself back on the market.

'And I always say to young hopefuls, tell employers what *you* can offer *them*, not what you hope they will give you – like you think it's time you got promoted/tried something different/had more responsibility/or (heaven help us) want to work in a nice office with interesting people. Which of course is what it's all about, but you don't need to let on!'

Added to all of that, it is a wise idea to find out about the whole financial package either before or during the interview. Bonus schemes, incentive payments, commission, subsidised meals, parking (if you're expected to use your car), payments for parking. What about mileage, wear and tear on the car, expenses if you have to take clients to lunch – what level of entertaining can you go up to? Some firms now expect you to clinch deals over a glass of wine or at a reasonably priced restaurant or even on the phone.

Personally I go along with that. The Business Lunch has always been a mystery to me, often boring, frequently unproductive, obscenely expensive and leaving both parties incapable of answering the phone for the remainder of the day. But if you think it's a part of the job that is necessary to your status and image (and saves you cooking when you get home), argue the point.

Holidays, time off, sickness pay, health insurance schemes? Try gauging their reaction to what they would do if you had to take time off because your child was ill. If you've negotiated a deal that means you work term time only, make sure they understand about half-term and the days when the school has 'stock taking' or 'retraining' or when it's hijacked for a polling station.

Check on overtime, weekend work (some women find this easier to handle while their partner or a relative is around to help with the children); sound out flexi-time, job sharing or shift work and the rates of pay for each.

Remember, you don't have to sound aggressive, suspicious or tough while extracting this information. I would not blame anyone for turning you down if you did.

Work out your questions carefully beforehand and preface them with phrases such as: 'I wonder if…' 'Some companies… Does this one?' 'I would appreciate it if you could tell me...' 'The bonus scheme sounds attractive…'

Leave at home openers like, 'What about overtime…' 'When do I get…' or 'I'm afraid I must insist…' And you cannot be serious if you even entertain such lines as, 'God, are you kidding…' 'Oh give me a break…' or 'Pul–eeese, get real will you'. Tempting though they might be.

Discover exactly who you will be answering to, which supervisor is in charge of your section and who is legitimately entitled to bawl you out or rearrange your working schedules. Get the levels of seniority sorted out (you wouldn't believe the strokes pulled by incumbent staff to unload dreary tasks on to the next, unsuspecting, one in), and make sure you have access to the person interviewing you, should you need it. Get the hours straight too. Some firms say nine to five and the entire dispatch section is on its feet at ten to, waiting to surge through the doors. Others say nine thirty to five thirty and really frown on you going dead on the dot, even if you are entitled to.

'It was hopeless. I'd worked it out that if I left at 5.30 I could get the 5.45 from Waterloo and be home by 6.30 to relieve Molly, my mother's help. But no-one else left that early, it was their winding down time. In the end I had to get another job.'
Christine, 34, solicitor's clerk, Addlestone.

'I used to leave a spare jacket over the chair so that they would think I was coming back. Or invent having a drink with a potential client, or collecting something. Anything rather than say I had to collect the kids.'
Beth, 32, market researcher.

Interviews are dependent on so many things connected with how you look, what you say, how you sit/smile/leave the room, that you wonder why anyone bothers to mug up on the company itself, and to hell with great qualifications.

Hard as it is, try not to move around too much, wring your hands, twist or toss your hair and, no matter how friendly the interviewer, it is not a wise move to curl your legs comfortably under you and settle down for a good old chat.

Qualifications are great, but often getting a job has been known to hinge on knowing everything about the company, the man or woman interviewing you and who their chief competitors are.

No-one expects you to say, 'I see you are having to reschedule all your loans after the Canary Wharf project ran into money troubles', especially if you are applying to be his PA. You will sound like a threat and no-one likes a threat around – especially if it's to their own job.

But something like: 'If you are planning to review office procedures I would obviously welcome the chance to be involved' or 'I really enjoy unravelling problems/typing/research so if anything like that needs doing I hope you will think of me'.

Make sure you know what they make, sell or produce before firing off your CV. It's easy to find out: ring customer relations or public relations in a big company; ask the switchboard of a small company. It can only help that you've taken the trouble to find out. Check the trade press and national press for recent information about the company, and try not to mention anything you remember Nigel Dempster writing about the state of the chief executive's marriage.

The mood of the interviewer, not to mention their personal foibles, and the whole hidden agenda of what they are looking for, has to be taken into account. Recent research findings showed that more than 55 per cent of prospective employers admitted that in the first two minutes of the interview what the candidate said came a poor second to how they looked.

So if you unwittingly remind him of his ex-wife, the PA who filed her nails all day, the accounts clerk who couldn't add up, then you're on a hiding to nothing.

We are not talking here about sexual attraction, or stereotypes for jobs, but human reaction to someone we think we are going to get along with. You may well find yourself sitting across the desk from the man who holds your future in his hands because, on paper, you sounded ideal; but human nature is fickle, and CVs are fragile, so personality is going to count for a lot.

Never slander other candidates. ('I hear you're also interviewing Jenny Murgatroyd. I had no idea she was out of therapy.') And no matter how jolly and friendly the interviewer is, avoid 'funnies' such as: 'I can type 20 mistakes a minute' or 'My shorthand's not too bad compared to my typing'. An air of enthusiasm is good, but squealing, 'Oh my God, I can't believe I'm even being interviewed' or 'I want you to know that even if I don't get this job, I think Britelite Batteries are just the greatest' is definitely overdoing it.

Sound interested and keen, but don't think you've got to 'project'.

You're not up for a part in 42nd Street, you hope to be the new co-ordinating manager of Fuseproof Fridges.

There are, of course, some bosses who still need reassuring about your status as a mother returning to work. Practise fielding awkward questions such as: 'What is more important to you, loyalty to your company or your home life?' There is no law that says you have to chose. Simply say: 'They are both important to me, as I'm sure your family and job are to you'.

Don't get drawn into one that starts, 'Between you and me, what is going to be the biggest problem for you working here? My wife works, I know how difficult she finds it'. Say as pleasantly as you can: 'I don't anticipate a conflict of interests. I'm very fortunate that I have such good back-up at home'.

Watch out for the one who tells you he/she has children of a similar age and you find yourself drawn into talking about them. Wonderful as they are, you will use up the interview time and leave the impression that you can think of nothing else. Find the opportunity to get the interview back on track: 'Talking of children, what is the company's policy about taking on graduates/school leavers?'

You may not get the first job you go for, and rejection is always a bummer, even when you know it isn't personal. But take it on the chin and don't be discouraged. You did brilliantly to get to the interview stage. Not everyone gets their first novel published, lands the leading role or hits the jackpot first time. They simply regard it as a rehearsal for the real thing – which is just around the corner.

NEW TECHNOLOGY
or WHICH BUTTON DO YOU PRESS?

'You could tell which screen was mine. The one with Tippex all over it.'
  Anonymous. Well, wouldn't you be?

Coping with Apple Macs, Word Perfect, Microsoft or any one of the seemingly zillions of New Age computers and programmes can be a nightmare for someone who for years has not been asked to handle anything more technically challenging than the pre-wash setting on the dishwasher.

VDU's, along with all the other high-tech systems of the modern-day office, can seem like another world to those who left full-time employment before the streets of most big cities had become overrun with motor bike messengers, when mobile phones were strictly for the police and a fax was surely something you put in a report. Along with what to wear, the prospect of mastering not just a new way of presenting work but what appears to be another language, is the single cause of keeping far too many women grounded in domesticity. However, on the whole, the business of new technology is nowhere near as horrendous as it might appear.

Remember when schools introduced the new maths system? The hideous embarrassment of not knowing how to do your child's homework. You got through that didn't you?

And what about when video games first crept in, and you found out your youngest could conduct a conversation on the conflicting merits of Spurs versus Arsenal while simultaneously scoring thousands of points on hand held pocket games with names like Donkey Kong or Pac Man. What were you doing? Still mastering the Rubik cube. Don't tell me, I've been there. And no, if you must know, I didn't.

Most companies have now switched over to new technology, and even the smaller ones with an even smaller profit margin have some equipment that requires training.

As with decimalisation and talking metres instead of yards, the success or otherwise of how quickly you grasp the basic fundamentals of operating a VDU generally lies in the person who trains you. Remember at school when you spent a whole year believing you were as thick as a post when it came to unravelling the mysteries of Pythagoras' theorem? And the blinding flash of clarity when next year you switched teachers and it sunk in?

Well, for some of you it might. The rest of us will now shuffle on uneasily.

So it is with computers and new technology. Most of us would not be innumerate or computer illiterate if the person sitting solidly beside us instructing us in where to find the on switch, was less keen on airing their scholarship on the subject and more aware of communicating it to someone who spends what free time they have on, in their view, quite unnecessary pursuits like going to the cinema, watching a video, catching an exercise class or putting their feet up.

These are the 'experts'. Every computer company has them. Some homes have them. Most, thankfully, don't. These are the people who love these machines and their capability with a passion and are genuinely bewildered when confronted by someone insisting through clenched teeth: 'Don't tell me what the computer is telling the programme to do. Just tell me which bloody button to press, will you!' These are the ones who sigh wearily as you gaze dumbly at the screen and say: 'Listen *again*. You must select COLUMNS STROKE TABLE which is, as I told you three days ago, ALT.F7. *Then* move to the cell where you want vertical text to appear and create a graphic block...What? But I told you only last week how to select graphics. That's ALT.F9...CONTROL...'

This is the standard answer, or something very like it, to 'How do I type the boss's correspondence and get a copy out of this thing?'

Personally, the ones I *absolutely* cannot stand, are the whizzes who come across to your screen to 'help', and then proceed to flick through the programme at dizzying speed, deftly manoevring that wretched thing called a 'mouse', leaving you utterly bewildered about how they managed to get the screen back to normal and just grateful that you have now relocated the urgent report you thought had vanished – along with the prospect of a job – forever.

Having been forced – and I do mean forced – to address myself to acquiring the knowledge a few years ago, I can only say that while I have not learned to love new technology, I have arrived at a grudging state of respect for what it can do, and would now resist any attempt to get me to operate anything that doesn't light up when I press the 'on' switch.

I suspect it's partly because I've got used to it, twigged in a very short space of time that the average user only needs to know how to turn it on, find a file, type a letter, save it (file it), print it, turn it off and go home for the night. A couple of days training should achieve that.

But will they tell you this? Are you kidding? Do you really want to deprive a man (for it usually is) who is deeply into gratitude, from his daily fix? And do you want to put him out of a job?

There are, of course, plenty of training courses you can go on, and if you are planning to return to work, and are constantly being told that they use Microsoft, Word Perfect, Quark, or whatever their particular fix is, then there is nothing for it but to take yourself off for a few days training.

Never lie that you can operate one of these programmes, let alone the machine, and hope that by some miracle it will work itself. It won't. There is something that destroys confidence when you are discovered furtively reading the 'how-to' manual in the Ladies, or that somehow fails to inspire hope in those on whom your future in the company depends if you are caught trying to kick it into life.

I grant you the temptation at times is hard to resist.

If you can't afford a course, then the best thing is to just come clean about it and see if the company run their own training programme or if there is someone who takes on the role of trainer. The problem with this – and indeed with most computer companies who supply trainers with the sale of their systems – is that they are not trained to teach. If only more companies would realise that just because that whizkid on the fourth floor could write a programme to revolutionise the City banking system while simultaneously hacking into the White House defence plans, this doesn't mean to say he has the skills to teach.

Two or three days is usually sufficient to master the basic rudiments of any programme, and most companies, particularly the bigger ones, are not going to turn down someone who is ideal for the job only because they are not computer-literate – although it certainly helps your case if you are.

'Once I had learned one programme, getting temp work was easy. The agency used to tell me in advance which system the next company I was going to were using, and I would mug up on it over the weekend.'
Julia, 42, secretary, Yeovil.

'On day one I felt like that lady who, when she asked for a pound of apples, was told we only do kilos now, so she said, okay a pound of kilos. I asked for another instructor. I just knew it wasn't me who was getting it wrong, he just couldn't teach.'
Jeannetta, 44, estate agent, Tenby.

'My daughter, who is fifteen, told me how to use it. She does it at school. She thought it was a real hoot. I thought it was just a huge relief having someone explain it in English.'
Marianne, 42, travel agent, Kilmarnock.

'The new secretary joined the queue at the paper shredder with some important papers. She asked the girl in front how it worked. Then she asked which button you pressed to get eight copies.'
Amanda, 43, secretary, Wisbech.

There is such a thing as RSI (Repetitive Strain Injury), and while it is unlikely that you will be a victim of this, it is as well to know that operating a VDU terminal for any length of time could (I stress only *could*) result in a painful hand or arm injury.
Why? Simple. In the days when we used typewriters, the keyboards and return carriage handle made us use our fingers and arms far more than a panel that requires little movement of the fingers and virtually none at all from your arms. You do not have to pause to feed the computer with paper or to rub out. You do not even have to move from your screen to take your work anywhere, you transfer it along the next stage of its life by pressing another button.
Just like driving on a motorway, when you should get out where appropriate and stretch your legs and move your muscles to prevent accidents, with a VDU you should give yourself a short break every so often, get up and move around to avoid damage to eyes and muscles. Most half-way decent companies have rules about breaks for employees whose job is entirely bound up in using a VDU, and while

there is only a small chance of it happening to you (unless you are in one of the high risk jobs where inputting reports and copy is a day-long job) do not allow anyone to tell you it's a psychological problem. There are quite a few people who say otherwise and one or two who have won compensation from uncaring employers who find it an inconvenient interruption to output.

Being armed with the power to crack every computer programme to come your way will certainly vastly improve your chances of work, but will it help you return to your old job?

Most women, having decided to go back to work, set their sights on the company or the kind of work they were doing before they took a career break. But, sometimes, re-entering the profession you trained for is no longer a possibility: incompatible hours, too many new techniques, shift work is now necessary, re-entry levels are wrong, maybe you yourself no longer find it as fascinating.

You may have to consider retraining for another branch of the same profession, or rethink the whole job, or indeed, go after a completely different one. Don't automatically believe that just because companies are cutting back, and it's a long time since you were a nurse/teacher/lawyer/secretary/journalist/go-go dancer, that you won't be able to slot in somewhere in your old profession.

However there are companies which encourage this. At SG Warburg, for instance, Richard Hardie has recently introduced a scheme whereby a few secretaries working for the company who take a career break to raise a family, can return on a temporary basis just to keep their hand in until they want to return to work full time.

'We keep their names on file and ask if they want to cover for holiday times for two or three weeks a year. This way they keep their hand in, and we get the benefit of using our own trained staff, so that we don't have to waste time explaining the company procedures to an agency temp. And because our work is confidential, we know our own staff are reliable.'

Remember that payments to a creche by an employer are tax free to the mother (or father). Most employers will not want to be involved in the direct arrangements or negotiations with the creche but ought to be happy to settle creche bills and deduct those amounts from the employee's gross salary. Richard Hardie has already used the scheme. What if your old job doesn't look so user-friendly any more? Does that mean you have to chuck your hand in and go back to re-runs of *Thirtysomething*? Not necessarily. You could always try a bit of cross-fertilisation: if accountancy was where you were at, all that detailed work might be as well suited to a bank, or research or working in a library. Your skills at communicating and organising could be very useful in **local politics** or in a **personnel** department.

And no-one who has been at home with small children can possibly say they haven't got a head start when it comes to knowing about kids. Have you ever thought about remedial **teaching** in your own home or **coaching** for exams? One of the most skilled and caring teachers I have ever met was a first year probation teacher at my daughter's school. After bringing up a family, she was determined to qualify. Who said it was too late, too old, no jobs? Write to: TASC, Room 4/17, Department of Education and Science, Elizabeth House, York Road, London SE1 7PH.

Public Relations is one area that doesn't necessarily need formal training but where good academic skills are a help. There are courses available and, while it is hard work, it is also good fun. Write to: Institute of Public Relations, The Old Trading House, 15 Northburgh Street, London EC1V 0PR. Tel: 071 253 5151.

Although a very competitive field, if you have an English degree or good A levels, **publishing** can be one of the most rewarding areas to work in. Write to: The Publishers Association, 19 Bedford Square, London WC1B 3HJ, for further details.

Retailing: Most major store chains will tell you there are no jobs, but what's to stop you having your name on the list and acquiring a few skills and some know-how in the meantime with a retraining course (details at the back of the book)?

While most **banks** seem to be reducing rather than recruiting, it is still worth ringing the head office of any of the Big Five and sussing it out for yourself. If you once worked for a bank, the obvious starting point is to ring the one you know. If you feel you've been out of it for a long time, see if there's anyone there who was around in your time (they may well be promoted to something grander) and get their advice.

Likewise, **nurse returners** in need of advice on opportunities and up-to-date technology, etc, should start with their old hospital or write to: Royal College of Nursing, 20 Cavendish Square, London W1N OAB.

Libraries are attractive propositions but the competition for jobs is fierce. However, nothing ventured. You may well have already got the qualifications they need (degree). <u>Write to</u>: The Education Secretary, The Library Association, 7 Ridgmount Street, London WC1E 7AE.

Don't automatically write off all your abilities, just move the furniture around a little. Not everyone who started out in life wanting one thing ended up doing it. The list is endless and includes: Fay Weldon who started out writing slogans for ad companies (Go to Work On an Egg was her immortal line); Glenda Jackson who was once an actress and is now a Labour MP; Betty Boothroyd who once graced the Tiller Girls and is now Speaker of the House; Angela Rippon who trained to be a dancer and is now adept at interviewing MP's and charming words out of mega celebrities; interviewer Lynda Lee Potter who trained to be an actress and is now a successful journalist.
Who says you can't change course? Remember, you are not making up for lost time; you are starting a new job and, who knows, a brilliant new career.

OFFICE POLITICS...
A RICH SENSE OF
RUMOUR Chapter Eight

An overtired two-year-old oozes more charm than the average office worker under threat. This is a fact, and one it is better to bow to before we go any further. Just like having a baby, you forget how painful it can be and go on to have another. So it is with office politics.

It is possible you've forgotten the heady relief when you opted to stay at home to care for the children yourself, knowing that never again would you have to suffer the paranoia of the head of sales after the MD kept you talking for more than five minutes in his office – or the grilling you got when you emerged.

Or the thrill when you discovered you were pregnant, and it wasn't entirely prompted by the vision of motherhood, but because you would no longer have to listen to the hysteria that erupted every time the manageress heard a client paying you a compliment, instead of her. (The type who blew a fuse so often, she was nearly always in the dark about office politics.)

Unless you arrive at your new office with a sign around your neck declaring yourself an incompetent mutant, then you are going to have to steel yourself for the threat you represent… at least until the rest of the staff get your measure.

The newest face represents energy and eagerness. Only you know that your youngest woke at 2am and again at four, and the desperation you feel trying to look bright-eyed when you reach the office at nine.

Any progress you make will not inspire your workmates to take you out to celebrate, especially if it comes within weeks (even months) of joining the company. It will be the signal that you are universally regarded as a slick opportunist, who uses charm, good looks and connections to get it going for you. The only place you should not use such dazzling qualifications is when applying to join the Carmelite nuns or some other career where modesty and self-effacement are considered advantages.

Hoping to win over the office or shop floor by sticking to your guns and being yourself is, truthfully, about as useful as spending a fortune on deodorants and still finding out you're resented.

Learn to play the game. Ask advice, be nice. Don't tell the firm's big player that you've heard the only impression he's ever made on the company was when he missed his chair at a board meeting – and don't warn the MD's secretary that her claim to be loyal only to her boss sounds more like a complaint than a boast.

Of course it's the truth... but I assumed you were hoping working life would lead you to live in the lap of luxury, get you out of the house, pay for a new car and the school fees, to generally fill the gap between what your ex gives you and what you need. Remember all those reasons when life at work seems unfair, unrewarding and only on nodding terms with truth or reality.

It is better to know now that in business the smart movers do not rely on talent but publicity to propel them ever upwards. I can think immediately of at least half a dozen people with delusions of grandeur who got there by planting the notion that they were good in the heads of those who matter. I expect you can too. Perhaps some of the names on my list are also on yours, but let it remain our secret. Libel laws work in this country. So, how do you get noticed?

Not necessarily through being industrious, but by obtaining a higher profile within the company. Getting yourself announced over the tannoy in the staff canteen is the oldest trick in the book. That way every head of department looks up as you stride through the room to take the call.

Always talk to any senior executive you meet in the lift: 'Excuse me, I'm Liz Newperson, I just wanted to say I like the new packaging/new uniform for the lift attendants, *loved* your appearance on Wogan'. No-one is immune to flattery. No-one forgets who doled it out.

Make sure you deliver internal memos by hand ('I was on my way to accounts, anyway'), join the social club, the works committee. That way you become a familiar figure around the building. And be sure that you are seen to be proud of your children. Plonk their pictures on your desk, casually mention their achievements (I didn't say a blow-by-blow account of Sam's performance in the Under Eleven's Five-a-side). Make it clear that you are happy about having them – as indeed you are – and that your domestic life is under control.

Too many women are afraid that in the eyes of others children equals problems; they avoid mentioning them at all in case it gives the impression they are basically a hostage to domestic life.

Likewise, a great many women who return to work after having children rarely imagine they will be considered for promotion. Frankly, the fact that in returning to the world of work they managed to find someone reliable to look after the children, overcame a natural instinct to buy another tracksuit instead of the chic little number they are wearing and resisted the temptation at lunchtime to remind their co-workers to eat their greens is, in the first instance, quite enough for most women.

And, as the days, weeks and months go by, if you're enjoying life and can afford to take on more responsibility, why not? But you must let it be known you're in the market for it. Simply hoping that someone will detect that you long to move up, to take over dispatch/become deputy chief supervisor, without you saying a word, won't get you far – if anywhere.

But, once having declared yourself a contender for any promotion going, you really do place yourself in the firing line. Are you ready for that? Because the sting of office politics is never more potent than when someone is getting on in the world.

Other women will tend to disguise their fury at being overlooked by being analytical and sympathetic about your success: 'Those contracts only went to her by accident, no-one else wanted them and, my God, rather her than me, poor girl'.

Interpreted correctly this means: 'What's she got that I haven't?'

Men are conditioned to dismissing female colleages as they (metaphorically) leapfrog over them ('and on to the boss' some might add) as part of the fashion for promoting women: 'Wouldn't surprise me to hear the office womens' collective voting him in as an honorary member' they snigger to each other. Or, with a sorrowful shake of the head, 'Funny, I never saw him as being afraid of women'. Even, 'My God, you can tell who wears the pants in his house'. And all because a reasonable, straightforward head of department thinks you're the best candidate for the job.

Salvaging their pride in the pub at lunchtime is number one priority, but this simply adds to their belief that the entire board are no longer playing with a full deck. 'Mad, unfair,' they mutter into their beers and ears of anyone unable to escape their whingeing, and promptly waste even more opportunities to get themselves promoted by embarking on a round-the-clock watch on your performance, just waiting to expose the flaws.

'When I walked in there was instant silence. The walk to my desk was ten feet. It felt like ten miles. And for what? I was just new.'
Jacqui, 29, stock control manager, Kennington.

'I lunched on my own for a month, wasn't included in the tea round, and had to collect my own post. All because, on day one, the department head suggested we had a working lunch to familiarise me with the department.'
Fiona, 34, corporate PR assistant, Belfast.

'The chief asked the four, all male, senior managers to take me to lunch as a kind of welcome. The office flirt was great fun. Of the others, one told me not to trespass on his territory. The other two looked about as welcoming as a bacon sandwich at a bar-mitzvah, ate in stony-faced silence, only asked me what I had been hired to do, didn't once say nice to have you on board, and left after exactly 60 minutes. My teenage children in a foul mood were charm personified compared with that lot.'
Michaela, 39, feature writer, Brighton.

Don't believe that you are safe at any level, from men or women, senior or junior, board room to post room. The ritual of office life is often more jealously guarded and certainly more rigorously imposed than within the most primitive of Amazonian tribes.
Give a good idea to the boss when you meet him in the lift instead of communicating through your supervisor, and you'll invoke instant purdah; ask the boss if the secretary can type a report for you without asking the secretary first, and the sound of bristles rising would be enough to make a hedgehog feel insecure; mention that you are holidaying at the same hotel as your boss, and they will ask the chief cashier for a breakdown of your expenses and to check you're not accidentally being overpaid; object to a colleague treating customers with a boredom that would make Sharon and Tracey look sparkling,

and the whole store may decide you're trapped in a time warp.

At this point you could well decide that to be successful at work requires unhingeing normality at reception and relocating it en-route to the station at the end of the day. You could also decide it's worth developing a rich sense of humour, get to like rumours, and get on with the job. Remember she who laughs, lasts.

There is no need to stay aloof, frown disapprovingly or chastise those who seem to believe it's a primary function of their job to destroy every good idea you ever had, and that it's their role in life to make sure lunch breaks, punctuality and holiday entitlement are not abused – except by themselves.

There's always one, jealously guarding their rights, but if you stop thinking their resentment is directed at you personally, you will realise that they regard everyone in the office as a potential threat.

Keep a sense of perspective and, if you want an easy life and a chance to enjoy each day, just smile sympathetically if someone gets a ticking off and indulgently at an unkind crack or to. Console a colleague by saying that you used to be in hot water so often your nickname was 'teabag'. Don't meet aggression with a martial blaze in your eyes, a heaving bosom and, dear God, never with a damp hanky pressed to your eyes.

Whatever the situation, bursting into tears won't help. It never does. Don't tell me. I know it's not distress. It's rage and impotent fury. But try telling that to a boss or co-worker already badly disposed towards you. In any confrontation, there is nothing more horrifying to most women (and, I'm reliably told, men too) suddenly to find your eyes stinging with tears and your mouth beginning to go just when you're trying to sound like a very together person.

So what should you do? Quickly invent a file you need to get, information to be picked up before you go any further. Say anything, but get out of the office for as long as it takes to draw a couple of breaths or to howl in the privacy of the loo. Having got that out of your system, go back and renegotiate.

However, if you really believe that tears streaming down your face will work in your favour, go ahead. Personally, I think only those blessed with the ability to cry like Michelle Pfeiffer, without sniffing loudly, their nose turning red and their cheeks going blotchy, might get away with it.

The rest of us may well win a temporary reprieve in negotiations, but only because most bosses have a horror of tears (that time of the month, neurotic, unbalanced, lack of judgement) and just want to get you off their back and into someone else's office, who will then do their dirty work for them.

Crying in front of a woman boss. Oh, come now…

When you disagree with your supervisor about the way the sales invoices should be processed and she hisses 'Listen you, I've been doing this job for 25 years', don't snarl back 'That just makes you very old, not very good'. Say instead: 'I realise that, which is why I was offering a suggestion, not a contradiction'.

Resist telling the head of department that a senior colleague is never there, even if it's true and you're having to do extra work to make up. You will have vented your anger and gained a negative. Bosses might listen, but they'll despise you more than the offender; after all, they will reason, who knows when you might blow the whistle on them, to an even higher authority.

Just leave the extra work, do your own, and say, 'Some of that needs a more senior decision/a more experienced hand than mine'. Leave it to the boss to find out where, and with whom, the 'experienced hand' is holed up, and to find out first-hand why the work hasn't been done.

You're getting zero information from your opposite number in the firm and it's reflecting on you. Stop asking and put it in writing – nicely. 'Miss Bigboots has asked for the stock control figures from Mr Smalltime. It would be helpful to have these today/lunchtime/now.' Copy the memo to your boss and hers, and sit back.

You hate sitting where you are, but you don't want to offend the person sitting next to you who doesn't mind offending you with explicit descriptions of their sexual conquests/noisy eating/body odour/political persuasion, by openly asking for a move?

Investigate where you can go. Find an A-grade reason for being there. Nearer to the library/within earshot of the boss/handy for taking in parcels. You might ask if you can use the empty desk while you finish a particularly tricky piece of work and then gradually stay there longer and longer, until everyone assumes that that's where you sit.

The extreme feminist who insists on referring to your former stay-at-home status as a domestic incarceration survivor (believe me that's a whole lot better than being called an unpaid sex worker), and who describes the smallest male courtesy as acquaintance rape, will be happy if you are quick to agree with her that the office groper is 'testosteronally challenged with hard to meet needs'. Telling her to 'kindly orientate herself elsewhere' (shove off) will only create an atmosphere.

There is also a hidden agenda in phrases that will become familiar to you and need absorbing. These are the top five:

We welcome suggestions from female employees.
(Easier to identify the trouble makers.)

Believe me, I understand, I have kids, too.
(Therefore I know you will be the same as my wife – neurotic.)

What does your husband do?
(Can I afford to exploit her?)

Was your divorce very expensive?
(Does she need the money?)

Do you take over your children at the weekend?
(Is she exhausted on Monday?)

To all these questions, you reply with a smile, that you sometimes find it tough going, but overall it really is less complicated than you thought. Give no-one food for erroneous thoughts – or gossip.

Office gossip is both the spice and blight of office life. It is impossible, unless you live a low-profile, bland kind of life, not to be the subject of it at some point.

'She said to me, "You know he's supposed to have slept with every woman in the company except one, and I bet it's that stuck up cow Jennifer in accounts".'
Mary, 42, secretary, Kelso.

91

Don't let it faze you. Enjoy it, even embellish it. Ignore most of it, and don't get paranoic. Only those having an illicit relationship might find it inconvenient. Gossip can give you the status of 'fascinating individual'.

Most gossip is harmless and at most will cause you just a few uncomfortable days, and only if it really is beginning to damage your reputation, or is wrecking your working life, should you take action. Why? Because office gossip (always high on content, low on facts) is the communication line to judging the mood of a company, whose star is in the ascendant, who is on the way down, who to confide in and who not to reveal your dislike of the Chairman to.

A certain amount of joining in the gossip is an act of diplomacy and, short of being a priest and hearing confession, it's very enjoyable. But always remember that the difference between news and gossip is whether you're telling it or hearing it.

It is no news to you that men are as bad, if not worse, at gossiping as women, so don't be lulled into believing that they are safer to confide in when you miss the kids and, as the rush hour looms, you think wistfully about enjoying an ice cream in the park after school, *Blue Peter* and *Neighbours* at 5.30. If you're going to have your confidences betrayed there's no difference between male or female colleagues. 'Choose your confidante carefully' should be writ large on every office door.

The only difference between men and women gossiping is that men call it 'analysing a potential office hiccough': eg, the chairman's secretary is sleeping with the managing director and the managing director's wife is about to find out about it. That, of course, is a problem for the managing director to deal with – but try telling a group of men, shivering with pleasure, that there but for the grace of God go they, and that it's not their concern.

'I never repeat gossip, so listen carefully the first time,' is a remark many of them sincerely believe exonerates them from dishing the dirt with the best of them.

It can help you get on – if that's what you want – and can even let you know when it's time to move on to another company.

Signs that someone is out to cause you trouble or has been telling outright lies about you as opposed to harmless gossip include:

persistent lulls in conversations when you walk into a room; discovering meetings too late to attend them; deliberately being excluded from inter-office memos that affect your job; catching the head of department glancing at their watch as you leave or enter the room. Someone's talking? You bet they are.

Don't let it continue. Ask to see your immediate supervisor or director and find out what the problem is. If they fudge and say you're imagining things, move on to new ground and say you're so pleased because you would like to ask whether you'd be eligible for a training course, want to talk about/get their advice on a new idea.

If you know for a fact who is spreading the rumours, simply shake your head sadly as you leave and say, 'I hate seeing Mary/Eric/Delilah so unhappy. Would you like me to talk to him/her, to see what's wrong?' At a master stroke you have shifted their view away from you (reasonable, enthusiastic, civilised) and on to a disturbed person – and you are elevated to the role of boss's emissary. Sweet revenge. Promotion before you know it.

Gossip is the barometer of office life, and can even occasionally give you the strongest clue you need about when to move in for promotion. But is promotion what you really want?

Stand back for a minute and assess what you really had in mind when you told your loved ones you were going back to work? Whether a high profile job *is* what you're after. If you have the back-up that takes the edge off the madness that frequently envelops the lives of working mothers, the life of a high-flyer might be for you. But it could also mean that your quality of life and your relationship with your partner and children will eventually suffer – because promotion might well mean that you will see even less of them.

This in no way means that women who return to work no longer have the same ambition as their male counterparts, or women who have not had a career break. It just means that it is no sin to want to stick with a job from which you already get enormous satisfaction and that doesn't totally eclipse your family life, and that you want free time to do other things/learn other skills, with your family or on your own.

So how can you tell? Assume that you are already working, and remember this is not a test but to find out whether you could survive in the office.

The acid test of office politics:
1. You discover a good friend at the office is your competition for a new promotion. She's tough, she's talented and she's suggested lunch today. Do you:
a) Accept lunch, taking the opportunity to wish her well in the job stakes, it's great women are being offered promotion and, if she's successful, you hope she'll consider you for her new team because you've got some great ideas. (All this, with one eye sizing up her words and appearance and what she's got to offer, of course.)
b) Accept lunch, but deliberately keep the topics neutral until coffee arrives, then say that, whatever the outcome, you're sure you'll still be friends and part of the same team
c) Test the waters by asking what she's going to wear to the interview and if she knows any particular line the company are looking for
d) Turn down lunch and turn nasty. Suggest the job probably isn't worth much if they're offering it to two women and hardly worth applying for
e) Withdraw your job application; you'd be too embarrassed to ask her to work for you, and too angry to work for her if you lose.

2. The boss's new live-in girlfriend has just been given a huge promotion and staff are outraged and mutinous. Do you:
a) Say 'business is business' and offer to do your very best work for her as she's a direct pipeline to the powers that be, and her good opinion is invaluable
b) Try not to ingratiate yourself with the new regime but distance yourself from the worst scandalmongers
c) Start flirting with another boss yourself because this seems to be the best route to power in this company
d) Spread a few nasty rumours as this might be a good way of toppling the upstart
e) Give up your dreams of job advancement. It seems a closed circle.

3. You have a woman boss for the first time. What best describes your first reactions?
a) Gender isn't important: there are innovative, considerate and decent bosses and disorganized, overbearing and difficult bosses of both sexes. You'll let her establish her credentials before you judge

b) A bit apprehensive; you want to be friendly so she feels at ease, but not too pushy, or she'll think that you think she can't handle the job
c) Cautious; this is a big job; did she get it by merit or by sleeping with the boss?
d) Uncertain. She may be very hard on her employees if she's out to prove how tough she can be to senior management
e) Feel hard done by; male bosses are so much easier to manipulate for sympathy. You just have to mention period pains and they give you the afternoon off.

4. In front of others at a meeting, an aggressive colleague remarks how attractive you are, just as you're about to start speaking. You suspect it's a ploy to put you off your stroke. Do you:
a) Reply: 'Thank you and what I'm about to say is even more impressive than the way I look'
b) Reply: 'Sweet, but I'm still going to have something critical to say about your department'
c) Answer: 'I do my best'
d) Blush and mumble, 'Thank you'
e) Ignore the comment but wish you hadn't worn such a short skirt, and now you've lost your train of thought.

5. You're having an affair with a divine fellow worker even though you both have partners at home. It's wrong but it's so wonderful you can't give it up. At the office do you:
a) Never spend any time together except when business or a meeting brings you together, and then never sit next to one another or make overfamiliar gestures
b) Never take lunches or coffee breaks together, or leave notes on each other's desks
c) Sometimes phone each other from across the office, or meet in the car park after work
d) Hint to workmates that you're having a passionate affair and they'd die if they knew who with
e) Touch their arm or ruffle their hair as you pass their desk: hang up on their partner when they call the office.

6. The new young whizkid vice-president has just become a father.
You don't know him well enough, but it's an opportunity to make
contact. Do you:
a) Congratulate him to his face and say you've sent flowers from the
entire department to his wife
b) Congratulate him to his face and say you've personally sent flowers
c) Send him and his wife a card at home
d) Take up a collection and buy a woolly baby blanket, but can't find
an opportunity to give it to him
e) Say nothing. You don't want him to think you're more interested in
babies and domesticity than work.

7. A job vacancy is coming up that would suit you perfectly, although
you're not the obvious candidate. Will you get yourself noticed by:
a) Approaching the manager doing the hiring, with a portfolio of work
and ideas, and personally tell them what you can do for the company
b) Write to the personnel manager asking for your name to be put
forward
c) Sidle up to the manager's secretary at lunchtime and ask her to
deliver a letter to her boss
d) Ask your present manager what they think your chances are and if
you should apply
e) Look at the list of candidates and wonder which ones you could
tarnish with a little grapevine gossip.

8. You've been offered the job and all is going beautifully. A year later
you discover you're pregnant. In another four months you are entitled
to maternity leave. Do you:
a) Keep quiet until 16 months and one day have passed, which means
there's nothing he can do, the law now protects you
b) Tell your boss immediately, saying this won't come between you,
your domestic arrangements are second to none
c) Tell them with tears in your eyes, implore them not to refuse to take
you back, say BigTime Incorporated has now become your reason for
being. After all, flattery is the best weapon
d) Test them out. Pretend you're asking on behalf of a friend and ask
what advice they would give her to hold on to her job. Then act on it.

They can hardly back off, if it's their advice
e) Divorce your husband. This isn't what you planned.

9. Your boss has made a serious error; senior management is fuming and the whole company knows it. Everyone's asking for the inside story. Do you:
a) Say, 'Why don't you ask them. It's their story to tell' and reveal nothing. But keep an ear to the ground for fresh opportunities in case the whole department's falling down with them
b) Refuse to comment, refuse to panic, but also refuse to go out on a limb for your boss next time
c) Volunteer information to senior management because you've always had doubts about the way the department was run
d) Tell the gang over drinks in the pub that you've heard some fishy rumours about what happened at your boss's last place of employment too
e) Question your boss bluntly in front of other employees believing that they're fair game.

10. You've just been made head of your department, something you've dreamed about. Now you feel you've arrived, do you:
a) Resist the temptation to crow and instead ask the best candidates who didn't get the job to work with you and build a super new team
b) Move your nearest rival along in a nice sideways shuffle but make sure they're always included in the weekly meetings, to soothe ruffled feathers
c) Move your nearest rival out of the department altogether and take a calculated risk they won't start building a rival empire
d) Inform your former office cronies you won't be joining them for lunch or gossip any more, you're far too busy
e) Create a huge fuss when you find out you have to share a secretary and you still don't have a reserved parking space in the car park.

Assessment: Could you survive in the office?
In each question a) is worth 5 points, b) 4 points, c) 3 points, d) 2 points, and e) 1 point.
40-50: You're expert at handling office politics and understand how

offices work. You know how important it is to get on well with the people you don't like, as well as the people you do. You've got a good understanding of 'the system' and are not intimidated by it, but know how to play by the rules to your own advantage.

30-40: There are few problems you can't handle; you're cautious and tend to wait until the dust settles or all the evidence is in before you commit yourself to a course of action or any one side. You're excellent at avoiding trouble and keeping your distance from ugly scandals at work.

20-30: You recognise how fragile office relationships can be and how dangerous, but you still have a lot to learn. Your first reaction isn't always in your best interests; you want the system to work for you but you need to learn judgement.

10-20: You're struggling and need some help. You need to sort out what you expect from the workplace and how you want to be treated – you've done some foolish things that reflect badly on your career. A little common sense might save it. Or a few good books on office management?

0-10: One of your difficulties is that you see yourself as a victim. You also don't see 'the big picture' – just your little corner of it. Perhaps an assertiveness training course or a few good books on office management?

Work is not necessarily the be-all and end-all of a woman's life. Whatever you find interesting – writing, running, dancing, exercising, archery, football, pottery, caravanning, tap dancing, reading, reciting, cooking, fund-raising – is all part of being a successful woman, not just what your job title says you are.

I've seen working mothers who were an absolute whiz at business and utter failures as human beings. And working mothers who were great at their jobs and turned down promotion.

I know many women who have gone back to work and love it just for what it is, and others who got such a taste for it they needed to hit the heights. Neither is wrong or right. Only you know if you're ready to be a star.

WORKING FROM HOME *or* YES, I'LL COLLECT YOUR CLEANING
Chapter Nine

Most people who set up office at home have more difficulty persuading the rest of the world that they are really working, than the businessman or woman whose working day routinely includes a three hour break for lunch.

There can't be a single person who hasn't at some time in their working lives felt the idea of walking from the breakfast table to their desk infinitely more entrancing than battling it out in the early-morning rush hour. And of course, as an idea, it most certainly is. It can be the answer to every woman's dream if she has small children and/or a husband who behaves like one.

For one thing, it's a lot less expensive than divorce lawyers, and for another you can work out your own schedule. At a stroke it dispenses with guilt and allows time for shopping, to collect the kids from school and to have supper on the table as his key turns in the lock.

All of those nodding with relief must, however, answer one simple question: if you still continue to collect the dry cleaning, sort out the jumble and make cakes for the PTA when, exactly, are you going to find time to work for money?

Working from home is only for those who are disciplined, regard it as work and can divorce domestic and social life from working life. To those who are not cut out for it, it can be about as attractive as ants at a picnic.

But, all kinds of people do it: accountants and designers, salesmen and singers, journalists and teachers, cooks and cartoonists, remedial teachers, piano teachers, photographers... So do typists, market researchers, dressmakers, hairdressers and historians. Selling children's clothes is popular and pottery is extremely possible if you've got room for a kiln.

However, while friends in salaried jobs are usually quick to point out the wonderful tax advantages to be had with such an arrangement, this is not so. The government and the Inland Revenue often seem hell-bent on wiping out any flair, ingenuity and, in the end, any *desire* to be a successful independent operator.

Try not to confuse working from home with freelancing; they are entirely different things.

Freelance writers working shifts on newspapers, film technicians working in studios or on location, temporary secretaries, auditors, agency nurses, models – none of them are employed full-time by anyone, but they could work every day of the year for several different companies in different places.

Working from home is when you physically do the work in your own home, with occasional sorties into the world, to deliver, collect or meet a business contact who, understandably, might be made nervous by constantly dealing with a disembodied voice down the phone.

You will find that the grey men (or women) in suits are always deeply suspicious, perhaps even a little envious, of those who work from home. So you must keep excellent accounts, and your temper, when dealing with the tax office, and remember that you have traded paid holidays, sick leave and company perks for the freedom to come and go as you will and life's financial swings and roundabouts.

Some work well from home; others just get by. The vast majority who do it well wouldn't change it for the world – until or unless someone comes along with a bigger, brighter, better deal that makes abandoning the freedom of working from home worth their while.

The truth of the matter is, however, that you will probably work longer, harder and more fruitfully than those who work nine to five for someone else. But before you start, take the following into account, or at least be honest enough to tell the truth...

Could you really be disciplined enough to work from nine to 3.20 when you must collect the children from school and then have them in bed at a reasonable time in order to finish off work that had to be put aside while you gave them tea and supervised their homework?

Are you really strong enough to resist a small child appearing around the door wanting to sit on your lap as you frantically try to finish typing up a feature, an invoice, a report, some research notes?

Are you strong-minded enough to threaten no *Neighbours* or *Home and Away* for a week when they keep raiding your 'office' for pencils, rubbers, paper, note pads. And which one of them, you would like to know, has been at the computer?

The truth is, can you really make the psychological switch from 'boss' to 'mum' in minutes and still finish that design/recipe/order? To be honest, and we are all in the same boat here, I never did any of the above at all successfully, but I still worked from home for an awful long time.

You will also have to learn to grit your teeth and smile bravely at those who do not understand – and indeed invade – your working life, just because it doesn't involve an early morning train, a boss – and a pension at the end of it.

I worked from home for 12 years while my children were growing up, during which time I earned an odder reputation than the one I suspect I have. Although they *knew* I was working, relatives and friends couldn't seem to grasp the fact that this meant I wasn't available to them for chats, lunch, coffee or shopping.

There was, for instance, the friend who tried to inveigle me into a local pressure group because, as she put it, 'Only those of us at home all day have the time to take on the road planning officer ', and spent days afterwards bristling with annoyance and telling all my other friends I was dead to any sense of community spirit.

And the distant relative who complained she had been trying to get me all day. 'I thought you worked from home,' she said irritably when I pointed out that a feature on drug addicts was impossible to research without going out and meeting a few.

If ever there was a work style universally misunderstood it is that of using your home as an office. Your children, honestly, will be the least of your problems.

'It's not proper work, is it?' is written all over the faces of those who cannot believe that anyone could want a job that doesn't include paid holidays.

'Must be marvellous in the summer,' they say enviously, implying that every time the sun comes out, work ceases.

'So lovely working in the garden,' and I would agree if landscape gardening was your forté.

Working from home conjures up the image of a day commencing at lunchtime and finishing – if indeed it ever gets under way – by four. It's a lifestyle for those apparently of Bohemian leanings: those work-shy (of course), bone idle citizens who do the odd scrap of work now and again, but only when dire necessity forces it or the bailiffs are getting nasty as only bailiffs can.

People do not see those whose office and home are one and the same, as being solid, hard-working, useful members of society – more as a convenient source of help when they want their children ferried to dancing lessons or to come to tea with yours (because 'You'll be there anyway, won't you?'), as a telephone answering service or a soft touch for coffee and sympathy when they drop in unannounced to tell you how being stuck at home all day is driving them round the bend.

You may, of course, wonder why any woman, with or without children, and in the name of reason, would want to work voluntarily from home when it's obviously such a trouble-strewn business. Not to mention acquiring a very dodgy reputation for leading such a weird existence.

After all, what is someone who claims to be working doing in Sainsbury's at ten in the morning? Working through lunch and possibly half the night, is the answer to that one.

What working from home really means is: missing out on the rush hour; having the freedom to say 'no' (it is, however, a fact that few people working from home ever do); no more wearying office politics; and being able to take more than an hour for lunch without getting dirty looks from those who had a sandwich at their desk.

You can live in those tracksuits, get away with two decent outfits, go back to bed after you've dropped the kids – if you've got a hangover – take a day off midweek, and be there if they all go down with colds, chickenpox or something they ate. You can alter your working life to accommodate half-term and the long summer break and feel virtuous about always being there when they get in from school.

It means not having to make excuses about leaving the office early because of sports day, prize giving or the Mother's Day concert, or worse, when the head teacher has sent a polite note asking to see you (twice the anxiety – getting time off and wondering what the hell has happened).

However, there are no pensions, no paid holidays, no sick leave and no guaranteed income. Feed-back comes only if someone phones you up to give you work or when the cheque for work you've already done – and which you've had to chase for weeks – arrives.

You will still need some help in the house – either collecting the children or getting rid of that pile of washing and ironing that could keep the Chinese laundry business going indefinitely.

Before you decide if you want to go it alone, there are 12 questions you should ask yourself first. Put aside whether it fits in with having children, because if temperamentally you are not suited for working from home, it won't do a single thing for you, the children or your nerves – don't let's even consider your marriage. An exhausted, discontented and now resentful you will see you both straight round to the nearest Relate office, long before the children kick up a fuss. So,

1. Do you like your own company?
2. Are you positive, quite bossy and the sort who likes to make decisions?
3. Are you easily dismayed by life?
4. If someone doesn't call you back within a day, do you feel rejected?
5. Do you like organising everything from a party to a school bring and buy?
6. Do you enjoy being at home?
7. Do you get bored easily?
8. Do you believe that if at first you don't succeed… complain?
9. Is your social life important to you?
10. Are you the person in your social group everyone tells their troubles to?
11. Are you conscientious about housekeeping?
12. How flexible are you? The school rings and says they need another pair of hands on the museum trip next week, and you've set that day aside to type up your report. What do you do? a) Refuse or b) Go.

If you answered yes, to (1), (2), (8), (9) and (12) – refuse, then you could enjoy, and make a success of, working from home.

People who work from home have to believe in themselves. That's why answering yes to question (1) is so important. You must be able to function in quite solitary conditions. Dealing with a quiet house, no-one dropping in for a chat, as well as being interested in what you're doing, are vital.

If you are everything that (2) asks, you should do just fine. You know what you want, and that bossy boots stuff (in reasonable measure) means you won't be fobbed off by a bored secretary to the person you need to talk to about getting some more work.

Complain? Who you? Never! Then don't try to work by yourself. But if you answered 'yes' to (8) you're on the right track to success, because on your own there's no big company structure to do the fighting for you.

BT haven't installed your phone? The stationers on the corner have printed your letterhead very badly? Atta girl. Refuse to pay until they do.

Yes, you've got to complain. The helpless 'little me' is a bit of a lost cause working from home. I would call it simply maintaining standards. However, I have met far too many people who called it and me, too many other things. Who cares? Just do it.

If you don't care about a social life, fine. But to feel inspired, invigorated and to keep sharp, you must be fond of an evening out. Getting legless in the 'Magpie and Stump' or quietly tipsy in 'El Corko's' is not really stimulating, is it? Neither is a clandestine meeting with your lover. But a girls' night out to giggle at the Chippendales can go down as research into social habits.

Social life means seeing a film, going out to dinner, having people round to supper, taking in a concert, a weekend away, going to the pub, or a wine bar, for a drink with your friends. It's essential – no it's vital. Not every evening or even every week, but a couple of times a month. Get a regular, trusted, babysitter and take off.

The benefits speak for themselves. It will keep your relationship with your partner in good nick, open opportunities to meet someone if you haven't got a partner and, most important of all, it will maintain links with your friends, so that you get invited out again, and so keep you in touch with the world.

And, lastly, if you politely but firmly explained to your child's class teacher (12) that you are not available for the museum trip this time, but maybe on another occasion, that's fine. If they sound frosty, politely ask her/him how they would react if *their* child's school asked for them to help on a museum trip during a working week. Precisely. Now let's turn to the remaining questions. If you said yes to all or even one or two of them, you really should think twice about trying to earn a living from home. Appealing as the idea seems and the perfect solution, it will create rather than solve problems. Being home-loving and/or needing to organise won't get you very far. You've got to have someone to organise, apart from the contents of your desk (which can be resorted to when life gets tough and you are looking for displacement activity. You know the kind of thing: 'I'll just tidy up all those paper clips and sharpen all those pencils before I get down to work'. The hell you will).

If you love organising you'll need a team around you and, if you wound easily, you'll have to remember that people in busy offices are not necessarily ignoring you when they don't ring back immediately – they're just busy.

Houseproud? Well, if you can't leave a jumble of cushions, newspapers and shoes in the living room for a couple of hours while you tackle 18 *Mousse Aux Fraises* that are needed for a client's dinner party... shall we leave it there? If, however, you want to have a go at working from home, make sure you have plenty of back-up to keep you going when the going gets overwhelming.

Part-time help – unless you can stop working completely while the children are around – is a must. Or at least some back-up if work takes you out and it occasionally clashes with school coming out. Can you really stop altogether during holidays?

Experienced workers from home eventually abandon asking kind friends to have yours home to tea. The investment in a regular part-time helper saves everyone's nerves, and the kids can come home to their own toys, books, TV or Nintendo and probably won't realise you're not around until you walk through the door.

I started, as most freelance writers do, with a typewriter, a phone and a list of ideas. Sounds impossible now with technology the order of the day, but it needn't be.

However in an ideal world, and if I were starting today, I would add an answering machine, a fax and a word processor. A good accountant is a must: find one who is just starting up and wants clients in his office not wall-to-wall carpeting.

Be very, very careful – and I can't stress this enough – about hiring or 'leasing' a fax machine with the option to 'buy' it at an advantageous price in two years time. The number of cowboys out there flogging them would fill Arizona, and just as many unsuspecting people are being harassed for money they never even knew they were agreeing to pay when they signed that innocuous-looking document.

The chances of any of them impressing a magistrate with their dodgy dealings are slim to zilch, even if they did get you into court, but it's a nuisance while those crude threats arrive through the post.

On the subject of money, early on in your career make a meeting with a reasonable bank manager to explain that your clients are not always prompt payers and so you do not want to swell his workload by having to fire off a letter to you every time you go into the red.

How do you get started and, more importantly, keep going?

Jobs are not just going to walk through the door. You must ask, advertise, look in the local paper, check with local groups. If you're good at dressmaking let your friends spread the word; if you're good at selling, tell Tupperware; if you're curious, ring up a market research firm.

If you like children (especially other people's) and you have the space, how about a playgroup or childminding? Ring the local Social Services department for advice on how to register. If you've got a great idea, but no money and no contacts, a small investment in an ad might produce results.

Make sure you can genuinely do the job from home. Brain surgery and anything that might affect your neighbour's rights (car parking/noise levels etc) aren't likely to get you anywhere except the magistrate's court.

Check that you're not breaking any by-laws and make sure you have your own 'office space', however small. The corner of the kitchen table has been known to produce a best-seller or a work of art worth hanging at the Royal Academy Summer Exhibition. (But far, far more have been binned.)

Always have a 'start' to your day, just as you would if you were working for someone else, and at least once or twice a month meet a work contact for lunch or a drink.

You must also read newspapers, watch the news and keep up with what's going on in the world; fashions change, new trends arrive. It's hopeless in business not to keep up.

Learn to say no to requests for help and make sure that if you need them arrangements for the children are reliable.

Finally, for all that tough talking about being your own woman, it really isn't fair to upset family life overnight, especially if older children are about to take important exams or the little ones are about to start school.

Take it easy, make sure it works. This of course does not apply if your partner is unreasonable, eg: he won't take his turn to cook supper, bath the kids or, when you ask for advice, snarls, 'It was your decision to work so you just get on with it'. My advice in that situation? Rethink your partner, not your ambition.

MUMMY, PLEEESE
DON'T GO! Chapter Ten

Heart-rending isn't it? Pitiful sobs as you try to disappear out of the door, on your way to your brilliant new career. This isn't what it was meant to be like.

Surely the scenario of your new working life didn't include a howling – no *screaming* – child, convincing you that everything ever written about selfish parents was surely based on someone just like you.

This is the child who, only a few days before, had seemed to prefer the new minder to you, waving cheerfully as you went. What you had expected, having so carefully selected the nanny or childminder and carried out a few dry runs, was a happy, secure exit from the house, knowing (your heart lurching) that life in your house would go on brilliantly without you.

This child is now approaching hysterics; your eldest is holed up in the bathroom or clinging obstinately to the leg of the table (having, you will notice, abandoned yours); the new nanny is not being much help, having decided from the outset that you didn't know nearly as much about children as you had led her to believe (parenthood, by the way, is no proof to a conscientious minder that you are any good at it); and you have certainly missed the train.

So you find yourself sitting at the bottom of the stairs, wearing your going-to-work clothes, with a now quiet child nestled on your lap, who is resolutely refusing to even acknowledge the minder's existence. Where have you gone wrong? What should you do?

This could be the time to invoke Plan B (see Chapter Six), when you call on that relative or friend you've put on standby – someone your child feels comfortable with and who will be willing to come to your house for a couple of days. But, even at this early stage, if you feel that the minder (in whatever guise – nanny, mother's help, childminder) is not right, let her go *now* and ask the angel in Plan B to fill the gap for a little longer while you find someone who is.

Children who are at school are slightly easier to organise. Arrange for them to go home with a friend for a few days while you sort out the problem. And involve your partner: it's just as much his responsibility as yours. This may be difficult because far too many partners still see childcare as your sole responsibility, but if it means him taking a couple of days of his annual leave to bridge the gap, then why not? If he refuses, I see nothing wrong in withdrawing all domestic support until he sees reason…

Making an effort to soothe and reassure your child will not give him or her a power complex, letting them think they can rule the roost. It will, however, reassure them that you are listening.

If the problem continues and you realise that your child is truly miserable at being parted from you, if school work is suffering, you notice childhood habits re-emerging, or your once-contented toddler is fractious and irritable, it might be worth rethinking the whole question of work and delaying it for a while.

If an older child suddenly starts saying they feel unwell, or becomes unusually withdrawn, don't start to panic. It could be down to many things, all of which have nothing to do with the fact that you work. Your 14-year-old, for instance, could be first-time smitten, by that blonde from the other school who gets on the bus. Or, as exams start taking on more significance at this age, they might just be in need of an extra cuddle or two. Finding the time to sit on their bed for a casual chat before you say goodnight might help, or a quiet word with a teacher; but you mustn't just ignore it.

One teacher I know admitted that the only age group she would never again teach was 14-year-olds: casting themselves in the role of the most misunderstood, neglected, much put-upon, tragic member of the house – correction, the entire world – comes quite naturally at this age. However, all this 'growing up' must be taken as seriously as common sense and your nerves will tolerate. In my view, if anyone needs quality time it's teenagers, if for no other reason than their need to screech at you that you don't, never did, do you hear, have anything like their problems. After they've slammed out, comfort yourself with the thought that your job is unlikely to be the cause of the fuss.

Whatever their age, with the vast majority of children there's usually a very resolvable problem; it is perfectly possible that any of the following are to blame:

1. You've done dry runs but wearing familiar clothes – the tracksuit. Your children know this spells Sainsbury's. They hate Sainsbury's,

they're glad you're not dragging them along. They know you'll be back shortly.

2. Your children don't recognise the chic red suit and four inch heels and wherever you're going they want to go too. You might not come back for ages.

3. When you wear those clothes you come back in a ratty mood, then Dad gets ratty and they can't concentrate on *The Bill* because of all that bad-tempered crashing about in the kitchen as you wash up.

4. Last night he was hiding his favourite Action Man from his older brother and put it in your bag. You are now taking Action Man to work. Give it back.

5. At playtime yesterday, the class sneak told everyone that you've lost all your money and that you have to go to work and that any time now you'll be put out on the street. Tell your child that you are planning to buy the complete Nintendo/give him the Liverpool Home *and* Away strip/get tickets for Simply Red/buy that toy car now instead of waiting for his birthday/take him and a friend to McDonald's – and you particularly want the class sneak to know. You must, of course, carry all this out. Expensive, but it *works*.

6. The class sneak has also told everyone that you are about to divorce which is why you are working. Tell your child that you and Dad will hold hands at the carol concert, stroll around the car boot sale arms entwined – and be sure to let the class sneak's mother know that you and Dad are planning a romantic weekend away now that you're in the money.

7. They don't want you to go without them. No way. Say that you were banking on them being at the station with the nanny/mother's help to meet you this evening, and how can they do that if they're with you? Make an elaborate plan to meet up, make it sound exciting. Decide which of you is going to buy the evening paper. Will you buy it at Waterloo or will they buy it in Lewis Meesons? Decide which sweets you both want and they can go with you to the corner shop to get them when you get in.

8. You're worrying that they don't feel part of your life any more? My God, they *are* your life. A child under five does not understand this kind of emotion. Get them to do something for you during the day. Something nice. Help bake a cake, draw a picture, sort out your jewellery/sewing/photograph box, tell you what happened in *Neighbours*/buy some flowers for the living room. Heap praise on them for doing it. (Blatant bribery is the only way with older children. They do not believe you are hysterical with excitement about the gingerbread men they baked this afternoon. Money would help.)

9. They don't know where you go each day. Arrange for them to see your office/shop/factory/studio. Choose a quiet time so that you don't disturb your co-workers. Lunchtime, or if the firm is open at weekends, maybe a Saturday. Make sure your boss or head of department knows you're doing this. All companies have security rules; your's probably won't be any different. If they can picture you at work this often resolves some conflict. For weeks my daughter thought I worked at the local station because that's where I disappeared to each day while, as a toddler, my son thought my husband (a film technician) was an airline pilot because we were always waving him off at airports when he went on location.

10. He's screaming blue murder because his older brother found Action Man in your handbag and won't give it back. Make him.

WHAT'S A NICE GIRL LIKE YOU...?

Chapter Eleven

Question: What is the difference between sexual harassment and flirting?
Answer: Sexual harassment is when you don't fancy them. Flirting is when you do.

It may well come your way. If you got a job because your sex life was boring and about as reliable as the weather forecast, you might be in for a shock at the reaction your mildly flirtatious manner invokes: what you wanted was a little light dalliance, but that may well be taken as a signal that you are game for a few more laughs than you had in mind.

If you got a job because you were serious about a career, wanted a new car, to pay the school fees – and are bewildered by how your perfectly pleasant daily greeting to the chief cashier has resulted in that worrying gleam in his eye as he personally delivers your pay cheque each month – then you should spend more time studying your manner and body language.

According to Jayne Monkhouse, spokeswoman for the Equal Opportunities Commission, a great many women returning to work really are unsure – having been out of the workplace for so long – what is considered acceptable behaviour and what merely makes them look prudish.

What you once thought of as no more than a friendly hug could these days form the basis of a massive lawsuit. Where once you would not have expected explicit language to be used in your presence it is now met with hardly more than a raised eyebrow – even by the office crone.

'He made more overtures than the Halle Orchestra' is a music hall joke, but not funny if it's clear he's tuning up to get you to join him for the finale.

So, what *is* sexual harassment, exactly?

Depending on your level of tolerance, attitude or beliefs, it can be offensive literature, posters, jokes or suggestions.

It is someone physically touching you, invading your personal space or leaving obscene messages on your VDU. It is making it clear that your progress is conditional on being 'nice' to him/her, or victimising you when you won't comply.

Sexual harassment is openly commenting on your physical appearance and encouraging other colleagues or subordinates to ridicule your distress, if this is the effect it has on you.

Could you cope with a groper without losing your job, resigning or ending up on the front pages of *The Sun*?

1. After a late meeting a male co-worker, whom you know slightly, offers you a lift home. In the car he makes a heavy and unprovoked pass. Do you:

a) Never get into this situation because you have your own car or always make your own way home, even if it means shelling out for a taxi

b) Shove him off, jump out of the car without giving him a second to explain, curse yourself for a fool and put it down to learning the hard way – and you now know something about him that you may be able to use in an office situation

c) Shriek, swear and utter a few threats, before getting out of the car and then phoning your best friend from the office as soon as you get home

d) Threaten to charge him with attempted rape or assault, and remind him of this next morning at the office after you've told your supervisor all about it

e) Cry and cry and cry until he gets nasty and tells you you're not a real woman if you didn't expect this after accepting the lift home, so you end up apologising to him.

2. You have a brilliant degree, several years' work experience and are obviously the ideal candidate for the job. The manager doing the hiring agrees you're just the person they're looking for, on one condition – that you spend the night with him. Is your immediate reaction to:

a) Burst out laughing and say, 'For one minute I believed you and thought you were going to risk your reputation and career

propositioning a woman who wouldn't hesitate to take you to the Industrial Relations Tribunal at the very least'
b) Say, 'With my qualifications I don't have to listen to this kind of bullshit; you've got 60 seconds to decide whether you want to hire me because I'm brilliant at what I do, or not'
c) Say, 'Sorry, from what I've heard other women say, you're not worth the effort'
d) Blush, be embarrassed and nervous and tell him you don't want the job
e) Debate with yourself right up to the hotel room door whether this is common practice and you're being unsophisticated not to have expected it, and now you're at the door, and now it's opening and now...

3. You're among a group of middle managers representing your firm at a convention, the highlight of which is a formal dinner. Are you wearing:
a) A chic evening version of your tailored day dresses, long sleeved and in a plain colour but dressed up with good jewellery
b) A suit with an evening blouse because you wanted to keep the emphasis on business, not the socialising or entertaining part of the evening
c) A cocktail dress which, although not revealing, is covered with more sparkly bits than you thought when you bought it, and is a bit shorter than you remember too. Still, it is an evening do
d) A long dress that you now realise is too full and floaty, more like you're off to the opera, than what is essentially a business dinner. You wanted to look sophisticated but actually you look overdressed, and like you're trying too hard
e) A real hot sexy number you picked up in a sale, because this is a big night out on the town and it's going to be fun. Of course you'll be shocked if any of the men make a pass at you because this is supposed to be business.

4. At the office Christmas party you get carried away and end up snogging with a manager in his office. The next day he asks you out, but you shamefacedly refuse. He keeps pestering you and pestering turns into hounding you. Do you:

a) Apologise because you're partly to blame for the wrong impression, tell him you regret the incident and hope you'll both just forget it
b) Tell him you had a lot to drink, behaved foolishly, and would he please disappear *now*
c) Threaten to complain to your supervisor if he doesn't stop bothering you, you can't owe him anything just because of a few party kisses
d) Avoid him as much as possible, feel guilty and sick when you see him, because after all you acted like a tart
e) Reluctantly accept his suggestion of a date because what happened was 'your fault' and you have to 'make it up to him' for leading him astray.

5. At the weekly meeting, the same male colleague always seems to find a seat next to you and rubs against your arms, legs, your entire body as you both rise from the meeting. You're going to have to do something about this. Do you:
a) Say very clearly and calmly next time he's close to you, 'Excuse me, but I need some space, you're too close'
b) Get to the meeting a good 15 minutes early and sit between two friends for protection
c) Say angrily, 'What do you want' – thus provoking a look of innocent surprise on his face, embarrassing yourself and causing a small scene 'about nothing'
d) Tell him to please leave you alone, which only makes him laugh to see how upset you are
e) Make a formal complaint about him to which he responds he doesn't know what you're talking about which then gets you branded as an unstable, over-sensitive trouble-maker.

6. A male co-worker has only one topic of conversation. He talks about sex suggestively at coffee and lunch breaks and while he's working. All the women in the department are becoming fed up and resentful. Do you:
a) Try and make lightly joking references to it that any sensitive person would pick up, such as saying if he doesn't find another subject of conversation you'll all talk non-stop about groceries, babies and diets and bore him to death
b) Completely, utterly ignore him and don't say a word to him, till it sinks in he's talking to himself

c) Ask him outright to change the subject, you feel it's inappropriate and objectionable

d) Request a transfer to another department to get away from him and his chatter

e) Consider, then give up the idea of making a formal complaint because you know senior management will consider nobody gets hurt by a bit of talking.

7. A male colleague is forever commenting on your looks, complimenting you on your clothes, saying what great legs you have, leering down your blouse, etc. What started as distasteful has become disturbing. When you've finally had enough of him, do you:

a) Tell him his opinion is a matter of complete indifference to you and try not to be alone near him

b) Turn rude and say 'who asked you?' when he compliments your new short skirt, hoping to embarrass him out of pestering you

c) Volubly and constantly comment on his suit and appearance in front of others to see if you can ridicule him into leaving you alone

d) Wear neck-high, calf length baggy shapeless dresses in the hope he'll find another more revealing victim elsewhere

e) Get horribly upset and look for work elsewhere: to complain about compliments seems silly.

8. If you feel you are being sexually harassed at work, you know that:

a) If you make a clear, unemotional and well-documented complaint to the appropriate person, action will be taken because the company has a clear policy on sexual harassment and other forms of discriminatory social behaviour

b) You can make formal complaints but they have to be backed by provable evidence, not just 'feelings', otherwise the company feels it gets embroiled in what are really personality clashes

c) There is no formal complaints procedure but your manager or supervisor is sympathetic and will deal with individual cases as they occur, at least taking the charges seriously

d) If you cry a lot a manager may sympathise and try and sort it out

e) There is no point in complaining about sexual harassment as it's not recognised as a valid complaint in your workplace, and besides, the guy you're complaining about is likely to be the boss.

9. At an out-of-town conference your formerly impeccably behaved manager knocks on your hotel door at midnight with a bottle of Champagne and says it's about time you two got together. He's obviously squiffed and looks more laughable than dangerous. Is your reaction to:
a) Tell him to go away and get some sleep and he'll thank you in the morning. You can tell the difference between harassment with menace and someone who has had a few too many and thought he'd try his luck
b) Tell him not to throw away five years of a good working relationship and say thanks but no thanks
c) Call him a fool and slam the door
d) Panic, slam the door, and call another female from the company also staying in the hotel and tell her what's just happened, forcing the incident into the limelight
e) Panic, call hotel security and get everyone involved.

10. Your supervisor suggests that if you want to get on in the company, you spend a little more time with him. Do you:
a) Tell him you're always interested in discussing business within working hours but don't believe in taking your work home with you
b) Tell him he's out of line and if he makes another suggestion you'll make a complaint
c) Rush off and tell three best friends in the secretarial pool you've been propositioned for which you get lots of sympathy and not a few murmurings behind your back that maybe you've been asking for it
d) Believe this is really how it works and you may have to put up with unwanted attention or worse to get ahead
e) Resign. The writing's on the wall. You can't win whatever you do.

Assessment: In each question a) is worth 5 points, b) is worth 4 points, c) 3 points, d) 2 points and e) one point.
40-50: You've got a well-balanced view of the working relationships between the sexes, recognising that people do get friendly, even fond of their colleague, but there is a difference between conviviality and harassment. You're not surprised men push their luck but you won't take any nonsense. You know your rights within and without the company and aren't afraid to exercise them. You're proud of the way

you can handle yourself in these difficult situations and don't feel embarrassed about demanding to be treated with respect.

30-40: You know you're entitled to work without being hassled, and that you should be treated well and with consideration, but sometimes you lose your temper or become over-defensive in your attempts to protect yourself. But you're nobody's fool and if you feel threatened or pressured you wouldn't hesitate to speak out.

20-30: You know you should be able to work without being molested, but the theory doesn't always translate into practice easily for you. You feel nervous about wounding male egos, but you wouldn't let serious harassment pass without comment, or action either.

10-20: You're not at your best when dealing with people under pressure or stress. You can't hide your own feelings well enough to deal with the problem calmly and coolly, and you sometimes misjudge situations. At least you're putting up a fight though, and a little more confidence in the working world may show you how to deal more effectively and less emotionally with harassers.

0-10: Oh dear. Harassment upsets you and you let it show. Nor do you believe there's much anyone can do about it. You don't feel you can deal with it very well at all and somewhere at the back of your mind is the suspicion that men can't help the way they act around women, so you feel guilty for causing any trouble. You haven't quite worked out how you want to be seen at work – as a flirtatious woman or a good employee, or if there's a combination of the two that's workable, and you're equally unsure of how to treat male colleagues. You need to know what the law says about workplace harassment, what your company's policy is, what the policy of your union is – if you have one – and sort out your own feelings. Every woman, including you, has the right to feel comfortable and not threatened by any man, anywhere, including the office.

It's younger women who seem to be the most vulnerable; older women, or those who are married, tend to escape direct harassment, but they don't always escape feeling uncomfortable or intimidated by the behaviour of male colleagues, and sometimes just the environment they find themselves in.

'Only about three per cent of cases brought to our attention involve women at management level. The vast majority are women much lower down the scale,' says Jayne Monkhouse, whose good-humoured, no-nonsense approach would convert any sceptic (including middle-class women, frequently journalists, unfortunately) who believes that sexual harassment accusations spring exclusively from the frenzied activity of the loony left and politically correct feminists – each and every one they imagine as being hirsute, overalled, Doc Marten-booted hags who have no reason to fear any approaches from red-blooded males, welcome or otherwise.

These sceptics define harassment as a friendly hug from a colleague, a kiss at Christmas or a risque joke which only the very prudish would feel threatened by. This view is of course, fuelled by, among others, right wing newspapers who want to sell more copies, and if I have any anger on behalf of women who suffer from the gruesome attention of what the PCs would term a testosteroned challenged sexual terrorist, it is that instead of helping eradicate totally unpleasant behaviour, by mostly men, they trivialise it. It becomes a not very serious issue. If only...

Now let's put all that into perspective. The vast majority of male workers, in my view and in my experience, are not arriving at work with the sole intention of harassing the female workforce with explicit gestures and even more explicit suggestions, which usually sound physically impossible anyway, and are genuinely bewildered at the very idea of one of their sex forcing himself on a woman colleague. Unfortunately there are some who do. Quite a few really. Enough to make it a problem. Because a lot of women colleagues are too embarrassed to make a fuss, usually take the first opportunity to find another job, and leave the company with no-one the wiser.

Jayne Monkhouse quotes the following two complaints which she has had to deal with as clear cases of sexual harassment – and any intelligent person would agree.

A thirty-five-year-old woman working for a tool manufacturers in the Midlands finally complained to the EOC about a male, slightly senior, co-worker who, having failed to get a response from her by muttering obscenities into her ear as he passed her work station, resorted to thrusting a certain part of his anatomy into her ear. This, not surprisingly, got her attention.

She complained. She won. He was fired. She returned to her job. She was ignored by her fellow workers who decided that she had 'ruined' the man in question.

The woman also eventually resigned. 'What she wanted was for the nuisance to stop,' says Jayne. 'That's all the vast majority of women finding themselves on the receiving end of such attention, hope to achieve.'

The second case involved a woman manageress at a supermarket in Portsmouth. She was fired for supporting the case of a young woman (also fired) who claimed sexual harassment by one of the kitchen chefs.

The supermarket also fired a male employee for acting as a witness and, mystifyingly, chose to ignore the fact that three other women had recently left their jobs to avoid being harassed by the chef.

The Industrial Tribunal who heard the case were shocked that the company had chosen to back their chef, in the face of overwhelming evidence that the chef had behaved 'inappropriately'. They promptly ordered the supermarket to pay out compensation of between £8-10,000 to the sacked employees, and left it to the management's judgement to decide on the fate of the chef.

The chef remained in the job. It is hard to understand why, unless you arrive at the conclusion that the management were sexually naive or perhaps terrified of the chef – who made no secret of the fact that she was Lesbian.

The problem with defining sexual harassment, according to Jayne Monkhouse, is that it is largely influenced by the attitudes and personal code of conduct of the person who feels victimised.

Sexual harassment comes under the Sex Discrimination Act and Equal Pay Act which came into force in 1975, the same year the Equal Opportunities Commission was set up, although the first case which clarified the law on sexual harassment was taken in 1986. Since then the European Parliament has issued a directive on the dignity of men, women and work which clearly signals that the situation is undesirable.

So one woman's (or indeed man's) sexual harasser, could in theory (but I reckon you'd have to be desperate) be another's date on Friday night.

'It's impossible to lay down a code of conduct that should be universally adopted because of the very different nature of strands of

121

business life,' explains Jayne. 'The media, the film industry – high profile jobs that attract ambitious and highly qualified women – might find restrictions that worked in, say, a factory employing a lot of women from a strong ethnic culture, as totally repressive and sometimes laughable.'

The whys and wherefores of who finds what offensive, are a complex minefield, strewn with moral codes, ethnic origins, political correctness and thinking between the generations that comes closest to lighting the blue touch paper.

Jayne recalls one case where a 19-year-old girl repeated to her aunt, some 15 years her senior, that her driving instructor had told her to 'be firm with the gear stick. Just like you would with your boyfriend's... ha, ha, ha'.

'Her aunt was outraged and wanted the driver dismissed,' says Jayne. 'However, her niece was horrified at her reaction and chastised her for being old fashioned. A lot of young girls feel intimidated in just the same way as a married woman returning to work after a gap – they don't want to appear unsophisticated.'

So there we are, and thus it is, with workplace life. Sexual harassment happens not just in offices, factories and shops, but in the police force, the fire service, hospitals and the army. Of the complaints received at the Commission in 1992, 20 per cent of the offenders were co-workers of the same grade, 15 per cent were the next level up, 35 per cent were supervisors, 12 per cent senior management, 10 per cent were clients and 8 per cent subordinates.

It is interesting that those who offended most were just one notch up from the person they were harassing. Talk about a little bit of power going to their... er heads.

The areas that *report* the highest incidence of sexual harassment (Jayne believes the EOC deals only with the tip of the iceberg), are the police force, the fire service and the army.

So what do you do when Arthur Wiggins, that respectable, upright deputy manager, suggests you might find your career prospects improve after an afternoon in a local motel, or the smoothie from marketing puts it about that you obliged him in the boardroom after work? They're both obviously sexually harassing you – unless, of course, you fancy Arthur Wiggins rotten and book the motel yourself, or consider the smoothie from marketing is helpfully improving your chances of a more varied social life.

You see?

What about this: The office Lothario sidles up to a woman colleague, having discovered her husband is often away for weeks on end.

'I expect you get awfully lonely,' he leers suggestively.

'Not *that* lonely,' she says briskly and pointedly, whereupon they part company without giving it another thought.

The same man approaches a secretary whose husband is also frequently away. She goes red, slaps him across the face. Thereafter, she refuses to work anywhere near him.

Codes of conduct can be, and are, influenced by the way some women approach working life. Career sex confuses the issue like no other. A rougher, tougher, approach to working life has become the norm for some – well quite a lot of – women.

Says Jayne Monkhouse: 'A woman who was working in the same office as a complainant was asked if she had ever been subjected to sexual harassment herself. She said she hadn't, unless you counted the times… and then reeled off a list that would have made an army sergeant feel intimidated.'

But is the man really entirely to blame, when his PA made the supreme sacrifice for an all-expenses-paid weekend in the Big Apple, for assuming her replacement will believe in the same route to the top?

If you feel you are being subjected to behaviour that makes you uncomfortable and you can't remove yourself from the immediate vicinity without losing your job, or altering your work conditions, you should do this:

If laughing it off, being assertive or telling him or her bluntly to lay off doesn't work, and you really do need the job, or like it, then start keeping a diary of the time, place and nature of the nuisance. Confide in another colleague in the office, in case you need a witness should it come to legal action.

A lot of women would rather leave their job than confront the problem or take the matter further. And it is perfectly understandable, because most of us just want to get on with our working lives and not be pitched into public battles which can be – and usually are – painful, which do not guarantee the result you want and which pose the dilemma at the end of how you can possibly continue working alongside someone who may, when it comes to the crunch, not lose their job.

But not confronting it is a shame because the offender gets away with it.

Being assertive is the best chance you have of stopping it. Making the offender aware that you *are* offended, and that you are prepared to say so loudly in front of colleagues, is sometimes all that is needed.

Many employers now have a procedure for dealing with complaints of sexual harassment. If you are harassed – use it. If no procedure exists, and your employer takes no steps to remedy the distress, consider taking a claim to an Industrial Tribunal. You could have a claim not only against the alleged harasser, but also against your employer for not preventing the harassment from happening.

Under the Sexual Discrimination Act your employer has a duty to provide a harassment-free working environment and could be fined up to £10,000 for failing to do so.

Back to our old friend money. Hit them where it hurts. No, not there – in their pockets.

Office affairs are quite another matter. Do not believe even for one second that yours will be different. It will end in tears, but if you haven't witnessed any clandestine office relationships before, or have never been involved in one, you won't believe it.

The fact that it isn't worth the risk and that your other half deserves better (unless you have cast iron proof that they are up to the same – in which case you have another problem altogether best analysed through Relate), will seem irrelevant to you, caught up as you are in the dizzy, heady sensation of new passion.

It is also an irrefutable fact that you will be the hot topic for the office grapevine and that you will be accredited with either being thick or being brazen by your colleagues – who can't believe you really think they don't know all about it. It is also expensive (all that money on new underwear), a great way to lose weight (all that agonising) and the fastest way to making yet another lawyer very rich.

It is the element of discovery, the sheer impossibility of it all coming to nothing, that makes it all the more attractive for some, the spice of life for others and the depths of despair and despondency for most.

Office romances are overwhelmingly conducted by couples, of whom one is certain to be married. Usually the man. But as statistics show that up to 40 per cent of married *working* women now claim to have had an extra-marital affair, it is safe to assume that the opportunity was created by a colleague with the same marital status.

If you're both married, and increasingly this is the case, you both have much to lose. Otherwise why all the clandestine meetings in empty offices, both parties rushing out on the pretext of buying the evening paper but really to make hurried arrangements for a five minute after-work drink in a pub near the station or that bar in Hyde Park, where you hope all the dark glass will make it easier to detect before you yourselves are detected?

Ninety per cent of your colleagues will twig immediately what is going on, despite all the elaborate precautions, and unless you are very, very lucky, your boss will too. That's unless the person you are having the affair with *is* the boss.

Falling in love with your boss is, of course, a mistake. Plenty of women do it. Plenty of bosses encourage it. Of course they do. How much easier it is to make someone who is besotted with them work late, for no extra money, sew on their shirt buttons, buy presents for their entire family, massage their ego (and much more besides) and generally organise their lives like a nanny/cum housekeeper.

The fact is that 99 times out of 100 he will stick with his wife (who has probably seen it all before) and, while you smugly think she doesn't know, she is equally and more believably thinking, poor you. Doing all the donkey work while she enjoys the money.

One hundred per cent of the time you will be the one to leave the job. One hundred per cent? Good grief, you don't think he wants his wife in the office keeping an eye on him do you?

Ponder these top ten lines from women involved in office affairs:

'It just happened.'
(So he hit you over the head and you woke up in that sleazy hotel in bed with him by accident?)

'It's not like that.'
(It is.)

'We don't want anyone to get hurt.'
(Someone will. Probably you.)

'He needs me.'
(He doesn't.)

'My husband doesn't understand me.'
(Oh Pur...leeese!)

'He hasn't slept with his wife for years.'
(Really? So his last baby was an immaculate conception?)

'He's never been unfaithful before?'
(Before he became boss and he's since made up for lost time.)

'How can something that feels so right be so wrong?'
(Oh, grow up!)

'I've tried to stop it, but what can I do?'
(Stop it.)

'Sometimes I hate myself.'
(Try hating *him*. Eventually it works.)

If you have a sense of humour, can accept the relationship for what it is and are able to shrug philosophically when it all ends, you may get away with it, get it out of your system and settle down to being happily married.

The chances of this happening are, on balance, more unlikely than of pigs taking to the air. The private hell known only to the dumped rather than the dumper, where unfaithful partners must retreat to lick their wounds, is about as desirable as toothache at two in the morning and about as much fun.

Unless you genuinely have met the real love of your life – and, like holiday romances, this is rare – ask yourself a few questions to try and put it in perspective:

Is it making you happy? Then why have you got a knot in your stomach all the time? If you are not eating, surely your husband/partner must wonder if you're ill? If he thinks it's the strain of going to work, why haven't you more to say about what happened at the office today, after all you were the one who wanted an interesting life? If you've told him it isn't all that interesting, what reason are you now giving for dolling yourself up every morning and arriving home in a trail of perfume and complete silence?

Why are you shouting at the kids?

Why do you jump out of your skin when the phone rings?

Why is it that, three months into this affair, your skin is looking blotchy, you're behind with your work, the department head is asking if you're finding the strain of working and family life too much to cope with?

How can you scream, yes, but it's *his* family not mine that's causing the strain.

How do you explain exactly why you are four hours late home when there's been no guards' strike and Waterloo wasn't evacuated, and what your car was doing at the station while you were apparently still at the office?

Why is your love object not having similar problems? How do you know he's never done this before? Where is it all going to end? How do you feel about single parenthood/being cited in a divorce?

What do you mean, you've lost your job? *What?* And your husband's done *what?*

Excuse me... Hello? Hello? Look, I was only asking... no need to walk off in a huff. Nothing to do with me. The last thing I want to do is intrude. After all, it's your affair.

DEAR CLAIRE, MARJE, PHILLIP – HELP!

Chapter Twelve

'**D**ear Claire,
I've been back at work for two months and I can't do anything right. Last night my daughter hardly spoke to me because I had forgotten to mend her jeans, and my son went to bed in a sulk because I screamed at him to tidy his room. I felt so guilty. It's not their fault I'm so tired, it's the job. Will I ever stop feeling like this?'
Phillipa, 35, store assistant, Essex.

Claire Rayner, columnist, novelist, TV personality, is charged with the need to live life to the full, and she does. Married to Des, a man she openly admits to being utterly dependent on, she is the mother of three grown-up children and has worked, albeit from home, since her eldest child, Amanda, was a baby. She has expanded and utilised, in every possible way, her training as a nurse.

More than almost any other woman in public life, Claire has worked to get rid of taboos, air grievances, discard rigidly-held views. She has campaigned tirelessly and vigorously for more understanding about how we view ourselves and, in particular, she's the staunchest champion of women who want to be themselves. Guilt she takes in her stride.

'Look, I felt guilty about whatever I did,' she says. 'I planned everything around the children so carefully, never missed a school event, always shaving time off everything I did to fit everything in.

'You can stay devotedly at home with your children and at 16 they will turn round and say, "What do you know about anything, you've never worked?" Or you can go out to work and they will say, "What do you know, you were never there?" It rends you in two. Whatever you do is going to be wrong.

'I remember Jay starting school, sitting at the breakfast table, his lower lip trembling away as he said, "Are you going out today? You won't be here? That's terrible". I was absolutely cut, but Amanda, who was 12, leapt in and said, "Listen, she may not be the best mother when you're five, but she's great when you get to my age".

'There were some awful times, like the day I was due to do a radio interview and Adam sliced the top off his finger and had to be rushed to hospital, and the time when Jay ran up a temperature of 102 and I was expected somewhere to give a lecture.

'Fortunately Des was always around as well, so we managed. Very early on, I also made my children self-sufficient. When they all reached their third birthday I said, "We are now going to play this very grown-up game, it's called washing up".

'I stood them on a chair and showed them how to do it, making a game of it, so that they became totally used to the idea. In fact both my daughters-in-law agree that my sons are excellent wives. They can do the lot. But, equally, Amanda can change plugs and deal with the engine of her car.

'I just wanted, as soon as possible, to be free from the burden of tidying up after them. And I desperately wanted them to be self-reliant as soon as they were able to be. I wanted them to be secure because I never had been.'

'Dear Claire,
I spent the weekend planning the week ahead. With two children, a full-time job and a husband who works away a lot, plus a mother's help who does what she's told but nothing else, I need to. Everything went wrong. I had no time, and no-one seems to think my time is important. Sorry to take up *your* time, can you help?'
Sharon, 36, home economics lecturer, Leatherhead.

'Time. There's never enough. And it's what every working mum needs,' says Claire. 'I had my time organised, it was other people who wasted it. Waiting in for the gas man, a domestic engineer not turning up, mucking up my plans. Working mothers are the greatest time-and-motion experts.

'In fact, my children were never a problem. It was other people. I was always finding ways to fit everything in to the time available. For example, when the kids were small they used to have big parties here, 30 or 40 kids would come.

'I looked around and thought, now what is the most time-consuming thing about a children's party. It was obviously laying the table. So Des and I made up food bags, just like goody bags, and marked each child's name on a bag and gave it to them. At the end of the party we just tipped the bags into a huge sack and that was it.

'In fact, I remember one winter being out in the garden with the kids making Swedish snow-houses – you know, you build a conical shape with snowballs and put a candle inside, they look smashing. Suddenly I saw a neighbour in floods of tears watching us. She didn't work, was at home all day with her children, and she said she never had time to do anything like that with her kids, and felt dreadful about it.

'She couldn't understand how, as a working mother, I could find the time. But the truth is, she didn't plan her time sensibly and I planned every day like a battle.'

'Dear Claire,
I earn more money than my husband. I thought he would be pleased. He isn't. At least, he says he is, but he still wants us to manage on his money, which is silly when we have three children and the whole point about me working is that it would help with holidays and stuff. I don't understand. Do you?'
Camilla, 40, market researcher, Winchester.

'Being the major earner goes deep with many men,' says Claire. 'It took Des some time to adjust to the fact that, for a long while, I was the major earner in our house. It started out with him earning much more, obviously, and then I wrote *Gower Street*, which really took off, and we decided that Des should now do his own thing.

'So he gave up full-time work in advertising and concentrated on being a painter. In many ways Des was always a New Man, a very active father, always helped in the house. We shared responsibilities, but we were creatures of our time, and at that time it was the man who earned.

'He also became my agent, which was great. We love being together. If it was just me and Des all the time, that would be fine. We don't need anyone else.

'The children are very amused by us. We hate being apart. We mooch around the house until the other is back. But, much as I adore Des, I would no more be satisfied with just marriage than fly to the moon.
'You ache for something more than domesticity. Going to the library, watching television, is not enough. Women have brains too, they need to use them. But if going to paid full-time work is going to cause absolute ructions, then think about it again.
'If the marriage is a good one, and the issue of you working is becoming a serious cause for arguments, rethink it. Seriously. Do some voluntary work. You can get more out of work than just money, and a good marriage is one worth preserving.'

****

'Dear Marje,
My husband is still sulking three months after I went back to work. He thinks I'm having an affair (chance would be a fine thing) and he now spends hours in the bathroom, rather than talk to me. Shall I give up work – or my husband?'
Anita, 42, wages clerk, Bermondsey.

Marje Proops, doyenne of the agony aunts and dispenser of the wisest words in print, has been agony aunt for the *Daily Mirror* for 39 years. With her dry wit and firm grip on how things really are and not peddling what we want to hear, there isn't a single facet of the lives of working women that she doesn't understand or hasn't advised on. She is in no doubt that women like Anita have by far and away the worst problem to deal with.
'When they return to work, the biggest hassle women have is with their partner,' she says. 'He can feel threatened because the malleable little woman he once thought of as being at home, messing around with the tea cups and the Hoover, is gone.
'He's used to making decisions because he's always been the breadwinner, and he doesn't like it when she wants to join in the decision-making.
'He likes the money, but he doesn't like the competition,' Marge explains. 'You see, once back at work, women stop being mere housewives. They start making friends with men as well as women,

and when they are expected to come home and revert to who they were, they think, "Bloody hell, I'm not doing that any more".

'Going back to work makes them aggressive, a natural progression from being assertive – which is what they think they have to be in the workplace – and they take this home with them. They're quite wrong, it's a fundamental mistake, but it takes time to realise that winning battles is not necessarily going to win the war.

'Women who write to me about their problems in going back to work simply want me to reassure them, to say, "Yes, go ahead, do what makes you happy". But I can't always say that. When it comes to the crunch, if you decide to go back, you pay the price. It is not as easy as it sounds.

'We hear an awful lot about the New Man, but he doesn't exist. There are just a few more men around who are more prepared to help, and most of them do not want competition in their own lives.'

Marje's own life was rivetingly chronicled in her recent authorised biography, *Marje: The Guilt and The Gingerbread,* by Angela Patmore, which detailed her own 20 year affair with a colleague while she remained married to her husband for the sake of their child. It tells how her own path back to the office door all those years ago was strewn with problems ready to trip her up.

'I worked as a freelance until my son, Robert, was six, then decided to take a job,' says Marje. 'One day he came back from school quieter than usual. It was only when I was putting him to bed that he suddenly said crossly: "Why aren't you like all the other mothers and stay home and make me cucumber sandwiches for tea?"

'I kept Proopsie [her late husband] awake nearly all night, sobbing and screaming, saying I was a terrible mother and I was going to give up work.

'Proopsie put it in perspective. He said the day would come when Robert would realise he had a better life by not having a discontented and repressed mother, bad tempered all the time because she is cooped up at home.

'Proopsie was sensible. He was also very good at sharing everything. But when it came to the day Robert was sick, I realised that, no matter how helpful, that was when the division of labour came to a halt.

'Robert woke up covered in spots and obviously had measles. Proopsie was very calm and said, "Now just get the doctor and don't

worry and call me at the office when the doctor has been".
'With that he swooped up his briefcase off the hall table where we
both dumped them in the evening – actually mine was a plastic carrier
bag – and went off to work.
'There was this amazing assumption that when it came to the crunch,
his work was more important than mine and even though I was
earning more than him, he just went off.
'I rang the office and said I wouldn't be in because of Robert, but I
was just seething with rage. Not because I had to stay with my son, but
because Proopsie hadn't even thought there was a decision to be made.
When he came in we had a blazing row and he simply couldn't
understand why I felt like that.
'Robert is just amused now at what went on. But he does remember a
lot of hostility and anger in his parents' marriage.'
Reassurance plays a big part in women returning to work and Marje is
very aware of the insecurities that beset women, particularly if the gap
between having their first child and returning to work has been
considerable.

'Dear Marje,
I'm in this office with a bunch of young girls who wear skirts that
leave nothing to the imagination. They all go off to lunch together and
I feel really left out. It's frustrating because I know so much more than
them, but you'd think it was the other way round.'
Sarah, 44, database clerk, Middlesborough.

'This is so common,' says Marje. 'Now it's the woman's turn to fear
the competition with younger women. There they all are with skirts up
to their bums, hardly any makeup – older women are very nervous
about that, they really worry about their appearance.
'I always say you've got to remember that the young girls you're
working with have a hell of a lot to learn from you, and the sort of
relationship you have with them will depend more on you than on
them. You have to be careful you are not too patronising. You can, in
reality, have chums who are 15 years older or younger than you, but it
needs goodwill on both sides.
'I get lots of letters like this one, from women saying they are
excluded; the younger women go out to lunch together; they don't get

included in the tea round; they all giggle together in corners.
'What they have to realise is that you should not go back to work and expect an instant welcome, especially if you behave as though you are the saviour coming to redeem the firm. You have to set out to woo everyone and I'm afraid that most of the time it's down to the newcomer to be seen to want to join in, not take over.'

'Dear Marje,
I'm in love with my boss. Last year I went back to work and there he was. His wife doesn't know, neither does my husband. I didn't mean to fall for him, I only went back to work because life at home was so boring. Honest Marje, he *really* understands me and the sex (albeit in his office which is a bit dodgy sometimes but we have nowhere else) is great.
I thought I was happily married – just bored. Shall I tell my husband? His wife? Leave? Stay? I didn't expect going back to work to be this complicated or miserable.'
Edna, 42, PA to stock control manager, Newcastle.

'The thing that is so interesting about a lot of women who return to work is that they say they are going back for commercial reasons, more money, companionship, to get out of the house – but they frequently end up in love with the boss,' says Marje.
'They don't know they are looking for an affair, but they are. They just want a flirtation to liven life up a bit and now they don't know what to do.
'Having an affair with the boss really turns them on. It's the power game, isn't it? And the boss isn't going to turn down the chance of an affair with a woman clearly dazzled by his authority.
'The younger women in the office have all told him to f… off when he's tried it on with them, and now here is this forty-plus woman, bored with her life, and he thinks oh, ho – and they're away.
'Then his wife finds out, and his lover is moved on to another department, possibly to a job she doesn't want, and ends up having to resign because she can't stand being ignored, and she can't make a fuss because her husband might start asking questions.
'What do I tell them? It's not the boss, it's the power. It's not love, it's boredom. Change jobs, not their husbands, and find a job that is more

interesting than the boss. If it's love it will stand the test of working for someone else. Usually it doesn't.'

****

'Dear Phillip,
My children scream when I go out and ignore me when I come in. Today my youngest's teacher asked to see me to find out if it's true he hasn't had a proper meal in weeks. Shall I change my children's school – or my job?'
Nadine, 37, medical assistant, Cranleigh, Surrey.

Phillip Hodson, counsellor, journalist and currently advising readers of the *News of the World*, has been committed to working mother Anne Hooper for 18 years. Both are counsellors and psychotherapists and have three sons – Anne's two boys now aged 23 and 21 – and their own 13-year-old. Phillip was at one time a father at the school gates – then a very rare species.
'Anne and I have always worked from home, so that we shared the jobs and bringing up the boys. Working outside the home was never a situation we had to deal with, but leaving the children with a sitter while we've gone out for a social evening was something we had to face very early on.
'Basically, a child who screams every day when his or her mother leaves for work has a problem. If he's continually anxious then something's up. Believe me, it is the exception, rather than the rule, if a child becomes that anxious. Mostly they give up yelling after about ten minutes and this doesn't last more than a day or two.
'But there are things you can do to prevent your child from making a scene or even feel like making one. Children are happy if they are told the short term, the middle term and the long term. In other words, keep them in the picture.
'If you're starting a new job, tell them at least six weeks before you start. Get them – and you – used to the sitter. They want to know, and should be told who, exactly, will be looking after them, making their tea, waiting at the school gates.
'After that, I think it's wise for working mothers to build into their schedule time to deal with any problems the child might have, and so

that they can be prepared if the child is anxious. It only makes things worse if you don't do this, because it increases the child's anxiety if he sees his mother looking tense when she clearly hasn't left time to cope with his problems.

'We make our children anxious. They learn from us. If we want easy lives and relaxed children, keep them informed. Once they know how their lives are going to be affected and dealt with, most of the incipient problems disappear.

'How would you like to start a job, not knowing the address, the name of the boss and what time you start and finish?'

'Dear Phillip,

I have married a man with a split personality. I have just realised this after 20 years of marriage. I discovered it a week after I went back to work. He said he would support me but he has suddenly become completely helpless. I wonder if he's been working too hard and now his brain is affected.'
Esther, 41, transport supervisor, Macclesfield.

'I wouldn't have thought so. He's just a typical man who doesn't know how to cope with all the changes going on around him,' says Phillip. 'Most men tend to see a part of their wife as their mother, and really need to be told what to do.

'Men like frameworks. I do accept some frameworks from Anne, and I do think it's a woman's place to be firm about her own intentions. I suggest being brisk, saying, "This is how things are going to go on now that I am going back to work".

'Work it all out and give a shape to the way all your lives are going to be conducted. Anne will sometimes say, "Get your diary out and put these dates in", and it's so much easier to know what it is you are supposed to do, what is happening.

'Men still tend to think of domestic issues as women's problems. They still have a need to be children themselves. It's a strange thing, but a man can more easily mend a washing machine than programme it for a family wash. But all these things can be learned, and should be.'

'Dear Phillip,

I want to go back to work, but my best friend says my child is not the

sort to put up with it. What sort? I've always been with him, never left him with anyone. No child could be more secure. What's she talking about?'
Kathleen, 29, Devizes, Wiltshire.

'I know what she's talking about,' says Phillip. 'Children who have had a poor experience of, say, hospital or a situation where they have been unwillingly separated from their parents for a time, are likely to be the most vulnerable, particularly if they were unprepared for the separation.

'And, curiously, children who have been overprotected by their parents, those who have their every move monitored, rushed inside if it starts to rain, everything done for them – washed, dressed, clothes picked up from the floor – are more likely to feel the lack of their mother (or father) in their life, if this constant source of support is suddenly not there.

'It is a good idea, if you want to return to work, to try and stop making your child so dependent on you. Simple things – teach them to dress, wash themselves, and don't make a fuss if they get dirty or behave as though major surgery is needed when they just fall over. Don't do for a child what he can do for himself.

'I remember when my son was about four, being poised on the top of a slide ready to hurtle himself down head first, something he'd never done before, and there was nothing I could do to stop it. So I just stood at the bottom, and waited to catch him, and my heart was in my mouth. He was fine. So was I, in the end. You have to allow your child to experience the world and, if you do, he is more likely to feel secure if you want to do something like go back to work.

'You need to feel encouraged about returning to work: someone to say yes, you can do it; no, you don't need me at your elbow telling you what to do; yes, of course you can manage a room full of strangers; you're great, clever, independent.

'It's encouragement that gets us all out into the world, including you and your child.'

'Dear Phillip,
I want to go back to work but I'm scared my children will start to hate

me and love the childminder – or even worse my mother-in-law who has always had it in for me. What shall I do?'
Elise, 34, Glossop, Derbyshire.

'The chances of your child transferring his or her affections from you to the childminder are remote,' says Phillip. 'Only children with a totally absent parent will build up a complete replacement relationship with the primary carer. But that isn't likely to happen. A lot of women continue to sacrifice their own feelings and needs out of a misplaced sense of guilt and this is not doing anyone any good.

'Children do not start to drift away from their mothers for no good reason and if you have prepared your child properly for your going to work, let him/her/they see that you like the sitter and that it's okay for them to feel comfortable, that's how it will be.

'If you continue to assess the effect they are all having on each other, you won't be concentrating on work and the whole exercise is pointless.'

SO HOW'S IT GOING?

Chapter Thirteen

Before you answer this – and mostly because mothers returning to work can't sort out guilt from real stress – let's have a quiet word on the subject.

Like Shirley Valentine, you may well have dissolved in the kitchen and reinvented yourself in the workplace, but that doesn't mean that despite having read this book, it's all going to be plain sailing.

The unknown lays traps for all of us, there's a banana skin around many a corner, and if you feel as though you've missed out a chapter somewhere that would have explained why, having achieved everything you set out to do – new job, great home help, money coming in – it feels like an alien being has invaded your body, and you are now someone else, take it easy.

You didn't skip a page and, no, you haven't turned into someone else. And you're not/won't be alone.

Around about the end of the first month back at work, your feelings about the conflict you've created (it's always *you* by the way, never your family, your job, the babysitter), start to get confused.

This is caused by two factors. The first is that business life in this country ignores family life. It is not rated as a situation that requires attention. (This is a scandalous situation and a subject for another book.)

But right now it isn't much help to you, because you are likely to be trying to handle the second factor: at this point, you see, you will more than likely start behaving covertly, and you can't work out whether this new pattern of behaviour means you are normal or completely off your rocker.

I once read about a woman who, having returned to work, took to checking if the fur on her child's cuddly toy was stiff from her child crying into it, and a single mother who advertised for a partner with a mother who would like to babysit. The stories are endless. Women who religiously continue to look up the number of the local takeaway, so that no-one will realise they know it by heart, and worse, take to changing their name over the phone when they call the pizza home delivery, just in case the neighbourhood gets to hear they won the 'best customer of the year' competition at Christmas.

There are other extremely nice, caring, anxious, mothers who give bath-time a miss, and only 'remember they forgot' after the children are in bed. Then there are those I was once shocked to read about, the ones who whip the thermometer out of their child's mouth before it can rise above normal – and then remembered that one of my best friends did it and defiantly claimed it still counted.

Others suspect that their children have twigged that tantrums, tears and temper are most effective if thrown at precisely 8.30am as you try to usher them out of the door and that immediate surrender, making no attempt to negotiate, giving in to all their demands, is a sure sign of guilt.

Stress is when you're screaming and beating your fists louder and harder than they are. Stress, ah stress. Great word. Covers everything from bad temper, to mental depression, to spoilt brat behaviour. But it is worth examining seriously just what it is and what it can do and, more importantly, what you can do about it – without losing your job, your family and possibly what's left of your mind.

'Guilty? Of course I feel guilty. If you sliced me in two, just like a stick of rock the word 'Guilt' would be written down each side. Now I hope to live long enough to be a burden to my children. It's what keeps me going.'
Margaret, 40, secretary, Kent.

'Some days I felt like a car… and the brakes had gone. I didn't give up work, I just changed my job.'
Jocelyn, 38, retail manageress, Londonderry.

'My husband would say: "It's that bloody job, doing this". And I used tearfully to agree. And then I realised it wasn't the job, it was no-one helping me at home. I said you can have a wife, mother and lover – or a housekeeper. Choose.'
Heather, 42, musician, Sussex.

I've witnessed the word stress hijacked by women whose situations could be described as merely aggravating or just plain inconvenient and, at the other end of the scale, applied to a working woman who was in the grip of a nervous breakdown and leaving her job or her family was not going to cure the havoc inside her poor mind. Stress wasn't in it.

Don't immediately leap to the conclusion that what you are suffering from is stress of the worst kind and, if you are, don't race to hand in your notice: most of the time you can control the chaos in your head. While I dislike the idea of the exhausted, overstretched, put-upon, guilt-ridden, working mother – and feel angry on her behalf – on the whole I prefer her to those working mothers, manicured to within an inch of their lives, who prattle on about quality time and try to pretend they know about commuting into the city, shopping at lunch time and the exhaustion, my dear the *exhaustion*, of arriving home to find their children already in bed but expecting a bedtime story.

Somewhere between the two is the ideal arrangement. Eventually you will find it, but it might take time. This is because nearly every working woman with children starts out by believing she is completely and utterly indispensable.

This is a notion fuelled quite shamelessly and untruthfully by those who will benefit most from making her believe this.

If you recognise yourself in this, and you are also extremely tired, start asking yourself a few questions: Do you take on more than you can handle? Does the first sound of raised voices have you galloping to be peacemaker? Are you always in a rush? When was the last time you read a book in the evening? Or stayed awake right through the ten o'clock news? Have you started to believe accepting offers of help is the first sign of being unable to cope? When was the last time you went to bed and found something more interesting to do than sleep? If you have so much to do, and feel that no-one else can do it, you will be rushing around so hard you won't have time to discover how you feel about anything any more. Rushing about creates an illusion of being aware, alert. But in truth it has the opposite effect: it makes you lose sight of everything.

Women generally tend to overstretch themselves. Sometimes they have no option. The average working mother's day can often be mistaken as training for the taking of a garrison town in the mid-West, and can leave not only the principal participants (the working mothers themselves) wrung out, but also the bit players (nanny, best friend, husband or partner) heading for the nearest haven of safety – a new job, another friend, and sometimes even another partner.

This isn't going to happen to you because you're going to recognise the signals before you've even reached the crossing. Here's how to find out approximately where you stand – or fall down.

Guilt versus stress:

l. When you arrive home from work, do your children rush to the door and greet you with:

a) Hi Mum, what happened to you today, guess what happened to me?

b) You missed a really important thing today so I'll tell you about it

c) Don't go to work tomorrow because something terrible might happen to me

d) If you love me, why aren't you here when I come home from school?

e) Who are you?

2. Now you're working, are you failing as a parent because:

a) You tell your children these cakes and biscuits are home-baked, but at Mr Sainsbury's home, not yours, ha, ha

b) Your children tell you never to buy them a dog because 'it would be lonely in an empty house all day'

c) At your child's birthday party, you don't recognise any of his school friends

d) Your child didn't volunteer you to help at the school fair because 'you can never do anything because you work'

e) Someone asks how old your child is, and you have to think for a minute.

3. It's never easy splitting yourself between the work front and the home front. How many times a week do you:

a) Drop off dry-cleaning on the way to work, shop in your lunch hour, pick up food after work, sew on a button at midnight

b) Schedule all the children's dental check-ups in your lunch hour and send them back to school in a taxi

c) Do Christmas and birthday lists at your work desk, and read work reports while waiting for the kettle to boil at home

d) Dream about work at night and daydream about home during the day

e) Feel you can't tell the difference between your boss whining for his report and your four-year-old whining for a story.

4. Christmas is approaching and your non-working friends are spending weeks making toys, decorations, dresses and puddings. How do you react to the festive season?

a) No problem – it's a pity it's not all done by you, but you shopped by catalogue in August and thank God for Marks & Spencer's

b) One day you plan to make something special and lasting for each child, but this year it's gift vouchers and book tokens again

c) Since 'everyone's' mum is making a stuffed animal this year, maybe if you sat up until midnight every night you could finish one too – if only your hands would stop shaking

d) You tell them they're lucky to get anything this year and book a day off sick to rush around the stores the week before Christmas. Now if only you could find someone to wrap it all

e) You're so tired trying to 'do' Christmas you cried last night and blew your nose in a bit of Christmas ribbon. The only consolation is it won't happen again for twelve months.

5. Your mother comes to stay and remarks pointedly that the children look peaky and your partner neglected. Your first reaction is:

a) You're glad you did that overtime, you can afford a holiday in the sun

b) They do look a bit pale, but it's mostly the lighting in the kitchen

c) They wouldn't look so bad if they got a bit of exercise doing a little housework or gardening while you were at work

d) It's true, but there are only 24 hours in a day and every one of them's full

e) If you think the children look peaky and neglected you should take a good look at me.

6. You feel you're running out of time when:

a) You get the store to wrap presents rather than do them at home; your daughter has outgrown the dress you've been meaning to mend for ages; your partner suggests making love and you say, 'Who makes anything these days, let's order it'

b) You're on first name terms with every fast-food delivery boy in town

c) You have to write the words 'relax and sit down' on the calendar otherwise you'll forget to do it

d) You wear dark stockings because you haven't had time to shave your legs for weeks, and long sleeved blouses because your armpits look like the Amazonian undergrowth

e) Your partner hasn't seen you naked for so long, he doesn't realise why you're always wearing dark stockings.

7. The worst thing that will happen if you don't get home for supper tonight will be:

a) The manager at McDonald's will think you're secretly in love with him, you're always dropping in so late and so alone

b) Your children will accuse you of trying to poison them again with Daddy's cooking

c) Your partner will be sulking and sex will be off the menu for a week at least

d) Your mother will call and hear the (not so) strange voice of the babysitter yet again

e) You'll have broken your promise to the children to be home.

8. Your children are asked what kind of job they'd like when they grow up. They say:

a) One where I can boss Mummy around and make her come home early

b) One where Mummy could take me to work with her

c) One that gave all the mothers a day off on sports day, Harvest Festival, the Christmas Carol concert and class assembly

d) One that won't make me fall asleep when my children are talking to me

e) I don't want a job. I want to be happy.

9. You're afraid working is making you lose touch with things at home because:

a) You only remember buying the children a puppy last night because there was a dog under the table

b) You don't recognise anything in the fridge

c) There is new wallpaper in the hall and you've only just noticed

d) Your husband has actually learned to cook

e) Your neighbour identified you as a 'stranger' to the police when you were wrestling with the garage door.

10. As you add up the pluses and minuses of being a working mother, you realise:

a) You've got a few more grey hairs, but a bit more money in the bank too

b) Now the children have a babysitter they like, the independence is great

c) Everything you've made at the office has been spent on pre-packaged food, childminders, extra clothes for work, bus fares, dry-cleaners and delivery services, from the grocers to the laundry

d) You can't remember the last time life didn't feel like a never-ending list of chores

e) You can't remember when you last woke up looking forward to the day, or left the office looking forward to coming home.

Assessment: In each question a) is worth 5 points, b) 4 points, c) 3 points, d) 2 points and e) 1 point. Add up the score.

40-50: You're quite guilty, as all mothers are, but you're coping well with the pressure and stress – it's giving you adrenalin, not ulcers. Your sense of humour helps; it keeps it all in perspective.

30-40: You definitely feel the pressure, but so far so good. Feeling a bit guilty about what your family may be missing makes you extra nice to them and you make sure they get some advantages from having a working mother – like a bit more money in the house.

20-30: Things are getting a bit sticky, and it's hard for you to tell the difference between guilt and stress. You're starting to think it's not worth it, and your family's probably decided already, no. But maybe a bit of reorganisation and co-operation at home could make it possible to work and not to have a grumpy spouse and resentful kids. Perhaps a list of priorities on the home front and then letting the rest of it go is worth a try – rather than trying to do everything yourself.

10-20: It's time to get help if you want to keep your job or your sanity. When you're this stressed out it affects the family, relationships, even your health. You want it to work, but it's all gone wrong. Time to build some de-stressers into your schedule, even if it's only an hour a week to yourself. And get as much help from your family and friends as you can – you're carrying too big a burden alone.

0-10: Stress has won the day, unfortunately. If you've boxed yourself into a corner, where neither work nor home life is enjoyable any more and everything merges into the same steaming pressure cooker, it's time to make changes. If financially you can – quit. You need to get your personal life sorted out before you take on responsibilities in the outside world. And you need to sort yourself out honestly too. If being away from hearth and home is this disturbing, perhaps it's the wrong thing for you to do. Your health and happiness, and the happiness of your family, has to come first. Or you could try a new, different job, and do the quiz again.

So now you know. And what can you do?
Quite a lot. Let go of all the things you can do nothing about. Does it really matter if the sheets have to wait another couple of days to be changed? Who cares if you have pizza three nights in a row? Is anyone really going to marry a woman old enough to be his mother, just because his own worked?
Just what do you do to relieve all the tension and get life back into perspective? A walk along a beach, in biting wind, belting out *Nessun Dorma* might do it. Take time off to watch a video, a really escapist one like *Brief Encounter* (unless it's a not-so-brief encounter you're escaping from) or *It's A Wonderful Life* (unless of course it's the overdue mortgage that's making you stressed).
Call a friend and have a character assassination session on your ex's new wife, go and see the Chippendales, get up and sing at a Karaoke night or plug yourself into your Walkman and get lost in Bruch's *Violin Concerto in F*. Okay, if you insist, Shakin' Stevens.
Even if you've always thought she was fair to meddling, tell your mother-in-law she's absolutely right, the kids *are* getting out of control, but you think a weekend under her eagle eye should sort things out, and pack them off to her while you spend the weekend in bed.
Shut the door on sibling rows and actually leave the house to go shopping/for a walk/to the hairdresser when your partner starts loading up his golf clubs, rings his best pal to go to the match, ransacks the fridge for his fishing bait, and assumes you are going to stay home all afternoon, minding the kids.

The point is, you've got to do anything that will make you stop. Stop thinking you've got to do everything. Stop feeling guilty. Stop getting stressed.

Okay, so what if it is the job. Rethink it. If you've been there for just two weeks and you feel as though you're already two months behind with your work and if the job isn't all it was cracked up to be, look for another one. One that has better hours, an easier location, a nicer boss. Maybe you should think about a slower track, not because you can't manage the fast lane, but perhaps, because you now have a family life, working doesn't seem nearly so important to you as it once did.

Equally, start asking yourself if your job is challenging enough. Life can seem wretched indeed if you are working alongside unmotivated people who think only as far as the next tea break or week off, and you get a real buzz from achieving targets set by the company.

Or it could be that you don't really want to work at all. You just thought you did. If you feel family life is suffering, examine why, and if you really have got so drawn into working life that you have less and less time for your children, then do yourself a favour and let up. Personally, I feel the same about men who think work is all, then one day they look around them and their children have grown up and they barely know anything about them. Then they plunge into a midlife crisis, behave badly and can't understand why no-one is sympathetic. Working is terrific, but being yourself and, even better, putting yourself first every once in a while, is not selfish, it's a hands-down winner, and that applies whether you work or not. Don't *ever* get drawn into the argument: who is happiest/most responsible – working woman or non-working woman? It is irrelevant and proves nothing. Guilt and stress afflict everyone and are no great respecters of personal circumstances.

Guilt is something we all have one way or another. Stress isn't a bad thing when it gets things done or makes us think, but who needs all that aggravation?

Pressure and stress are different. One you can live with and the other you need like a hole in the head. So let's get this straight. Guilt is when you find yourself passing off as home-made the cake you bought at the bakers for the school Christmas bazaar, or you tell your beloved (who is looking a bit plump round the middle) that he's losing weight in order to take his mind off the fact that you fell asleep as he was describing the evasive action he took to avoid the contra-flow on the M25 tonight.

But when you drum your fingers and there's no music playing, and your answer to 'Have a good day' is 'I have other plans', you are not having a good time, are you?

Rethink it all if the stress applies to you. But keep going if you merely feel guilty: remember a mother's place, working or otherwise, is in the wrong, especially if she's getting it right.

But mostly, put this question to those who aren't helping you to be a working mother. It's very simple. You ask them straight. Do I really have to give up me, to be loved by all of you?

Should you still have doubts about exactly how qualified you are, read the following job description which is reproduced with kind permission from the Department of Employment booklet *Back to the Future* published in association with Woman's Hour.

Housewife Required

An opening exists for a talented, dedicated, conscientious woman to organise a chaotic household and its inhabitants.

The candidates should be attractive and poised, able to produce a stunning four-course meal with no apparent effort and simultaneously clear up the debris left by four assorted children, two cats and a dog who spent the afternoon rolling in a field full of cows.

She must be prepared to act as protector, mentor, nurse and nanny to the children, offering them unlimited affection and understanding, mingled with precisely the right quantity of discipline. Despite being knee-deep in nappies with regurgitated lunch dribbling down her shoulder from the baby she cradles, and various unspecified substances being systematically rubbed into her skirt from the mouth and nose of the toddler at her knee (who constantly asks 'Why?' and must be patiently answered), she must never appear anything but calm, nor lose her allure for her poor care-worn husband.

In addition, the candidate should be adept at sewing, cleaning, pre-school educational activities and socialising. The successful candidate will have the opportunity to put her landscape gardening experience to good use, provided that she does not neglect her other duties. She should also be willing to join local committees and stand for school governorship (these may only be carried out if she can find a babysitter. At other times she must be prepared to babysit whenever her husband wishes to go out).

She must be prepared to get up every hour during the night to see to the baby, interdispersing her care with settling the other children and tending to her husband's needs. (Applicants who suffer from recurrent headaches need not apply.)

Candidates should be willing to find paid employment to supplement the mortgage, dovetailing it with her responsibilities at home so that the latter does not in any way suffer.

Experience in management, financial budgeting and product selection are essential, and counselling skills are an advantage.

A driver's licence is preferred, since the candidate will be expected to provide a taxi service for her own and others' children.

Hours: Flexi hours are available, provided the candidate is willing to work any twenty four hours out of twenty four.

Salary: Variable to non-existent, but not negotiable – the job should be its own reward.

I rest my case.

HELPLINES –
AND NOW FOR SOME
ACTION...

In the space of one book it is difficult to encompass everyone's individual needs. One woman's problem may well be another's solution. An organisation that meets the needs of the domestic life of one family could be lacking in diversity for another. The following is therefore offered as a range of options from which you can pick and choose. Don't give up if one organisation doesn't seem right for you: an investment in research at this stage could save you much on trial and error.

Having been down the road of returning to work, I have based much of this book on my own personal experience and that of my friends. I have tried, therefore, to push you in the right direction, but there is absolutely nothing to beat a personal conversation with the right agency or department, or an expert in the field, to understand and advise on your own individual needs.

A great many women I spoke to in the course of preparing this book said they found not just the titles of women's organisations, but the organisation itself, intimidating and 'not for someone like me'. Although I believe some women's groups are invaluable, I understood what they meant. It is for that reason the following list confines itself – as indeed does the book – to practical and emotional advice and a first port of call for returners.

However the purpose of returning to work is not to add to your problems and the aim of this book is to help get you there, so a few names and addresses plus telephone numbers (correct at time of going to press) may well be very useful to you.

Childminders:
Find the number of your local DSS office in the phone book. They will put you in touch with the relevant department who keep a list of registered childminders.

Childminding in Business,
National Childminding Association,
8 Masons Hill,
Bromley,
Kent BR2 9EY.
Tel: 081 464 6164
Advice on how to select a childminder (rather than nursery care) and also the association to which most good childminders belong in order to protect and promote their interests.

Childcare:

The Lady Magazine,
39-40 Bedford Street,
London WC2E 9ER.
Tel: 071 379 4717
Published every Tuesday, it is the most widely used source for reputable agencies for nannies, mother's helps and au pairs. Even so, check details and references yourself. Write to place an advertisement yourself; telephone orders are not accepted.

Kids' Clubs Network,
279-281 Whitechapel Road,
London E1 1BY.
Tel: 071 247 3009
Promotes out of school care and play facilities for children.

Nursery World,
Unit A,
The Schoolhouse Workshop,
51 Calthorpe Street,
London, WC1X OHH.
Tel: 071 837 7224. Fax: 071 278 3896
Another good source for finding the right help. Published every week, you can fax or phone copy as well as sending it by post. Check first what their rates are.

Single parents:

Gingerbread,
35 Wellington Street,
London WC2E 7BN.
Tel: 071 240 0953
For lone parents and their children. Gingerbread is famous as a
starting point for advice and support for any lone mother who wants to
return to work. Their experience and networking skills are invaluable.

National Council for One Parent Families,
255 Kentish Town Road,
London NW5 2LX.
Tel: 071 267 1361
Objectives explained by its director, Sue Slipman: 'Our return to work
courses grew out of a direct demand from lone parents. We started
with welfare benefit courses designed to help lone parents survive on
benefit and to support self-help information and advice projects. The
lone parents on these courses have told us that they do not want a life
of surviving on benefit. They want to work.'

Retraining and general guidance:

Pepperell Network,
The Industrial Society,
Robert Hyde House,
48 Bryanston Square,
London W1H 7LN.
Tel: 071 262 2401
The Pepperell Network is a national network providing advice on
training and career development for women. Individual membership is
£50 per year, which covers four Network meetings and six issues of
Peptalk magazine. For further information contact Caroline Gielnik or
Jo Gardiner, National Campaign Leader for Individual Development
and Equal Opportunities.

Careers for Women,
1st Floor,
2 Valentine Place,
London SE1 8QH.
Tel: 071 401 2280
A professional guidance service for women of all ages. It offers
individual careers counselling and psychometric testing which
assesses an individual's abilities and aptitudes. It is able to provide a
wide range of information from how to present yourself to a
prospective employer to producing a good CV. It will also advise on
long-term career options and is often able to come up with new ideas
not thought of by individuals.
An appointment can be made in London or a representative will visit a
reasonable size group in other parts of the country. A one hour's
careers interview for someone currently unemployed will cost £38.78.
Psychometric testing costs £160.98 for unemployed women. Other
tests are extra. Write for an information pack.

Working Mothers' Association,
77 Holloway Road,
London N7 8JZ.
Tel: 071 700 5771
This is a self-help organisation for working mothers of all ages and
their children. Through a network of local groups it provides an
informal support system. It will advise on childcare provision and get
mothers to share support, advice and information. Groups run
themselves and are not controlled by the WMA although advice is
available if needed. Groups are funded individually and the structure
and activities are determined by local members.
A newsletter and contact with other groups is provided, together with
a handbook which covers many aspects from finding a child carer,
costs and so on. There are also workshops and conferences. Annual
membership fee £10.

Guidelines,
Sanderson CBT Ltd,
Sheffield Science Park,
Howard Street,
Sheffield S1 2LX
TEL: 0742 768682

The Department of Employment developed the Guidelines project as a guidance system for women returning to paid employment. The computer assisted system is designed to be located in public places where women throughout the UK would have easy access to it – libraries, supermarkets, and so on.

It is designed as a friendly, easy-to-use system where anyone without any prior computer experience can find out about suitable careers. By answering some simple questions about yourself, you will be provided with suggestions tailored to personal skills, needs, experience, aspirations and personal situations.

Women and Manual Trades,
52/54 Featherstone Street,
London EC1Y 8RT.
Tel: 071 251 9192
Provides information and advice about and for tradeswomen. It is for women interested in working or training in the trades. Runs conferences and training sessions. There are workshops in Bristol, Sheffield and Birmingham, but it will handle nationwide enquiries. Backup support is provided for self-employed tradeswomen. There is no membership fee, but a subscription of £2.50 is charged for a newsletter. Write for an information pack or free register of names of tradeswomen available for work.

Women and Technology,
Drake House,
18 Creekside Betford,
London SE8 3DZ.
Tel: 081 692 7141
and
Women's Computer Centre,
Wesley House,
4 Wild Court,
London WC2B 5AU.
Tel: 071 430 0112
Advice and courses on new technology.

Launching a new career or updating an old one:

Women Returners Network,
8 John Adam Street,
London WC2N 6EZ
Tel: 071 839 8188
Publish *Returning to Work: a directory of education and training for women,* £12.95, plus postage and packing, an up-to-date comprehensive directory in education and training, as well as listing colleges and organisations nationwide.

The Women Returners Training Consultancy,
33 Lausanne Road,
London N8 OHJ.
Tel: 081 986 5105
Runs variety of courses for women returning to work as well as providing, if you want it, a more personal one-to-one advisory service.

Vocational Guidance Service,
83 High Street,
Hemel Hempstead,
Herts HP1 3AH.
Tel: 0442 68645
Offers individual career assessment and puts you in touch with the organisations that can lead to the right job for you.

Problems in the workplace:

It may also be necessary for you to get help with some problems when you get back to work. Finding out your rights re maternity leave and sex discrimination, not to mention sexual harassment, for instance, can leave you battle scarred but not defeated if you know where to go.

Any problems you have at work, of a contractual, discriminatory or sexual nature, can be dealt with in the first instance by calling:

Equal Opportunities Commission,
Overseas House,
Quay Street,
Manchester M3 3HN.
Tel: 061 833 9244

More specifically, get hold of an extremely well researched document produced by the Policy Studies Institute, 100 Park Village East, London NW1 3SR. *Maternity Rights in Britain*, the experience of women and employers, by Susan McRae and W W Daniel will give you sufficient background to the climate to fight your corner if needs be.
Copies can be obtained from BEBC LTD, 9 Albion Close, Parkstone, Poole, Dorset, BH12 3LL. Credit card orders on Freephone 0800 262260.

A booklet published by the Institute of Personnel Management, *Statement on Harassment at Work*, can be obtained from IPM House, Camp Road, Wimbledon, London, SW19 4UX. TEL: 081 946 9100. If you have any doubts at all about the rights and wrongs of sexual harassment, this is what Roger Farrance, President of IPM, has to say: 'No-one should be worried about going to work because of fear of harassment, bullying or abuse. An environment in which harassment occurs reflects as badly on the organisation as on any of the employees within it. The IPM deplores any kind of harassment and urges employers to take steps to ensure the dignity of employees and customers is not abused.'

N&P
ASPECTS OF LIFE

Aspects of Life is a series of publications designed to help people to respond to the changing circumstances which they face as their lives progress.

In an entertaining and down-to-earth style the Aspects of Life Series seeks to encourage readers not only to tackle their responsibilities in a more fulfilling way, but also to enjoy the stimulus of new challenges.

The subject matter, which at present ranges through home life, leisure and work is being chosen to recognise the diversity of experience and opportunities which individuals and families may encounter.

This pioneering venture by a building society draws on N&P's unique experience in responding to customers' requirements, helping people to achieve a better quality of life.